BEAUTIFUL LESSON ABOUT KIMOYO

By: Kofi Piesie

© Same Tree Different Branch Publishing

Kofi Piesie/Mossi Warrior Clan

Copyright 2020 by Kofi Piesie Research Team

All right reserved. No Part of this book may be reproduced or transmitted in any form or by any means, electronic or mechanical, including photocopying, recordings, or by any information storage and retrieval systems without the written permission of the publisher.

Printed in the United States of America

Table of Content

Acknowledgment..................................5

Preface..9

Introduction....................................11

Foreword: Okomfo Nkuu A....................13

Chapter 1: Kimoyo............................21

Chapter 2: Africa The Place Of Humanity And Kimoyo..32

Chapter 3: Oral Traditions....................46

Chapter 4: Supreme Deities and Lesser Deities..57

Chapter 5: Rites of Passages..................76

Chapter 6: Rituals And Sacrifices............94

Chapter 7: Sacred Object and Sacred Places..114

Chapter 8: Music..............................135

Chapter 9: Masks..............................149

Chapter 10: Why We Turn Against Our Traditions......................................157

Acknowledgment

First and foremost, I would like to thank my Ancestors who came before me. Jerreh len jeff suma ai maai mi contan si yen torop.(Honor our Ancestors, and we respect you and proud of things you've done.

As I put this book together, all I could hear is my dad's voice in my head saying I tried to research where I am from and our history when I was your age. When my dad was searching, there weren't many resources available, or just hard to get access to those resources. There was no internet, no online books stores, or social media outlets to access information.

My dad's voice in my head inspired me to write a book for those who tried and came up short, those who do not know where to start, those who started but confuse and want an understanding of their ancestor's way of life call Kimoyo.

I want to thank Benjamin Njie and Asar Imhotep for inspiring me to do this book, so I dedicate this book to these two brothers. I greatly appreciate what both brothers do and what they both represent, and how they carry themselves.

Mossi Warrior Clan, Kofi Piesie Research Team, I am grateful to be among you, great men, and it is an honor and pleasure to know each of you. Thank you, brothers, for being my friends.

Asar Imhotep

Asar Imhotep is a software developer, Cultural Theorist, and Africana researcher from Houston, TX, whose research focus is the cultural, linguistic, and philosophical links between the Ancient Egyptian civilizations and modern Bantu cultures of central and South Africa.

Asar is the founder of the Madu-Ndela Institute for the Advancement of Science and Culture. He is the author of several publications.

Benjamin Njie (Blak Pantha)

Benjamin Njie (Blak Pantha) is a Pan Afrikan, Lecturer, a proud member of many organizations, and Co-founder of the Mossi Warrior Clan.

Benjamin Njie (Blak Pantha) is an advocate of

African Spirituality and uses the principle of these ancient practices to solve problems within the black community and in the diaspora worldwide.

Benjamin Njie (Blak Pantha) is the author of two Pan Afrikan Journals and two children's books.

Preface

For those that might not be familiar with me, my is Kofi Piesie, and I am a member of Seshew Maa Ny Medew Netcher, Mossi Warrior Clan, and Kofi Piesie Research Team. The Seshew Maa Ny Medew Netcher is a group that is striving to be a true and royal scribe. We study the writing script of the Remetch call sesh medew netcher and the language ra ny Kemet. We have transliterated and translated numerous texts from Egyptian steles and facsimiles.

Mossi Warrior Clan is a group that studies West African culture and traditions in-depth, but we also look at East, South, Central, and North African traditions and culture as well.

Kofi Piesie Research Team is a group of individuals studied in various information topics, such as Arab culture, historical Moors, African History, writings, languages, cultures, traditions, science, and North, South, and Central America history. Each group has published plenty of books throughout the years, so we do not just talk; we produce good works for our people and the next generation behind us.

This book, Beautiful Lessons About Kimoyo, has been a dream for me. My inspiration and determination to start and finish this book have been my people's shame because of propaganda and flawed narrative about our Ancestors' life.

Introduction

Africa is the cradle of humanity, and the life of humans and human Ancestors started in many processes and stages. Our species, homo sapiens, begin to travel and migrate because food lacks in many places. As homo sapiens begin to try to understand their environments, such as fire erupting rocks, water falling from the sky(rain), life, death, birth, animals, plants earth-shaking (earthquakes) and their purpose, so they begin to ask and ask about those things. Our ancestors were trying to understand, and over time they begin to answer those questions with myths and folk tales.

About 10,000 to 15,000 years ago, humans started to mold nature to their needs and agriculture, which cultivated plants and livestock. This method became the critical development and rise of human civilization.

These civilizations began to produce culture, i.e., rules, morals, ethics, and conduct.

Kimoyo has evolved and spread slowly for millennia; stories about gods, spirits, and ancestors have passed from one generation to another in oral mythology. Singing, dancing, drumming, sacrifice, pouring libations, establishing sacred places, rites, and rituals Introduction also became a big part of the culture.

Every ethnic group in Africa has developed its onset of beliefs and practices. Despite their seemingly unrelated aspects, these systems have standard features, suggesting that Africans have formed a cohesive tradition we call Kimoyo.

Foreword

By Okomfo Nkuu Apem

"It is a good sign of the progress made in civilization by the native-born negro race that they speak of the Africanians with much of the contempt with which Europeans talk of Negro"- Charles Lyell 1855- Enslaved Africans in America did not leave the spiritual hierarchies of Africa behind when they were dragged from their homeland by slave traders. On the contrary, elements of the old spirituality survived in the American South. Though African religions were largely frowned upon by colonial authorities, they survived and adapted, enabling enslaved practitioners to enjoy a degree of freedom by conducting their social and private lives—people whose lives were controlled by intrusive owners.

On the African continent, spirituality was simply an outward expression of culture, heritage, and reverence to ancestors (some deified). Outside of elaborate rituals only known to initiates, these outward expressions were shared with the greater community in the form of art.

As in Africa, and as well in the Americas, the descendants of enslaved Africans continued to gather in secret for rituals and, in an exoteric fashion, teach the community at large via art.

Over the centuries, the iron fist of oppression has crushed some Africans to the point they no longer recognize themselves; even when confronted by the most precise mirror, they deny the reflection therein.However, all isn't lost, and a large number who labor under the fist have stood firm and planted seeds for a future harvest.

The Iron First of oppression codified their death blows into laws they imposed upon a people already crushed. As explained early, Art was the medium by which spirituality was disseminated to the masses.

Music was the center of this action, and the drum was the head of every assembly. The drum also acted as a voice for the voiceless. In the 1800s, due to countless waves of African armed campaigns of freedom, the Drum was outlawed by many southern states.

In the Negro Act of 1740, we read pervasive these laws were to Africans attempting to hold on to their spirituality:THE NEGRO ACT OF 1740 XXXVI. And for that, as it is necessary to the safety of this Province, that all due care be taken to restrain the wanderings and meetings of Negroes and other slaves, at all times, and more especially on Saturday nights, Sundays, and other holidays, and their using and carrying wooden swords, and other mischievous and dangerous weapons, or using or keeping of drums, horns, or other loud instruments, which may call together or give sign or notice to one another of their wicked designs and purposes; and that all masters, overseers, and others may be enjoined, diligently and carefully to prevent the same.

Be it enacted by the authority aforesaid, that it shall be lawful for all masters, overseers and other persons whosoever, to apprehend and take up any Negro or other slave that shall be found out of the plantation of his or their master or owner, at any time, especially on Saturday nights, Sundays or other holidays, not being on lawful business, and with a letter from their master, or a ticket, or not having a white person with them; and the said Negro or other slave or slaves met or found out of the plantation of his or their master or mistress, though with a letter or ticket if he or they be armed with such offensive weapons aforesaid, him or them to disarm, take up and whip.

And whatsoever master, owner or overseer shall permit or suffer his or their Negro or other slave or slaves. At any time hereafter, to beat drums, blow horns, or use any other loud instruments or whosoever shall suffer and countenance any public meeting or feastings of strange Negroes or slaves in their plantations, shall forfeit ten pounds, current money, for every such offense, upon conviction or proof as aforesaid; provided, information or other suit be commenced within one month after forfeiture thereof for the same.

Laws of this caliber lingered on long after the men who penned them went to their grave, so too did African spirituality. In the early to mid-1900s, North America witnessed an explosion and flourishing of African American Art; this period was dubbed The Harlem Renaissance. During this period, Jazz emerged, capturing the ears and attention of Africans and European Americans alike. The critical eye of established European commercialized music fixed their gaze on Jazz, using a mixture of inherited fear

of retribution and limits understanding of African spirituality. This newspaper article from 1920 reveals the fear and contemporary attitude of Europeans towards African spirituality and, by default, African music:

"Harmony Expert Says Jazz Is Relic of Voodoo Chants Chicago, May 9. According to Dr. Frank E. Morton, chairman of the Music industries committee, Jazz is the evil spirit of music in speaking at the opening of the Music trades convention here today."Jazz," said Dr. Morton, expresses hysteria and incites to idleness, revelry, dissipation, destruction, discord, and chaos. It accords with the devastating, volcanic spirit that has burst forth over the world in the last six years.

"Rhythm and musical vibrations swayed the half-savage voodooists like a powerful intoxicant. It shows the extreme to which musical vibrations can control human nerves when improperly employed.

Jazz is bad music, but the difference between the incantation-crazed fanatics and the patriot or soldier stirred to noble action by music Is a difference in the music itself. "Jazz is compounded after the same formula as the voodoo chants.

" During the period of The great African migration in North America (1890 to 1970) we see a rebirth of African pride in the northern United States. As people migrate, they brought with them not only material possessions but also culture and spirituality. Many headed north for the mythical land of "Canaan" they've heard so much about growing up listening to those elders, who had stories of people who escaped the chains of slavery for freedom in the north.

Unfortunately, the north had mastered the Art of covert oppression, and these people would experience some semblance of freedom. The oppression wasn't only confined to policing where one could be at a given time, but their spirituality was also hindered and infringed upon. In this newspaper article from 1898, the columnist shared some insightful commentary concerning African Americans in northern cities:

"The police officials tell me that four out of every five-colored persons Arrested in the big Northern cities carry voodoo charms about them and are most anxious to keep these articles when searched. I know of a colored jockey-one of the best American professional riders of his day who never takes an important 'mount' without first of all consulting a proficient in the cult of voodoo.

It is next to impossible to crush out voodooism by force. One can only hope that the spread of education among the colored people will, in the long run, destroy this survival of their primitive African days."

The Inter Ocean(Chicago, Illinois) February 27, 1898, Sun • Page 25

Now, more than ever, the importance of keeping African spirituality alive should be in the front of the mind of all Africans. We should sow the same seed from which we came for those who are to come after us. I stand with my brother (the author) and do bear witness that he is of good character, and his labor in educating Africans is indeed a Noble and honorable one.

A study of each element in Kimoyo is, therefore, the ultimately study of the people's themselves in all the complexities of both traditional and modern life."

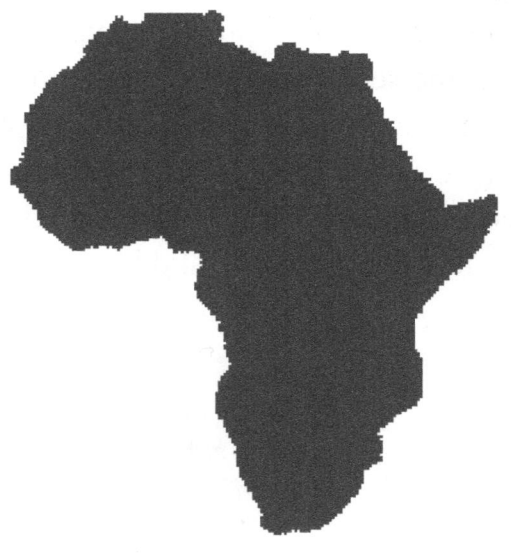

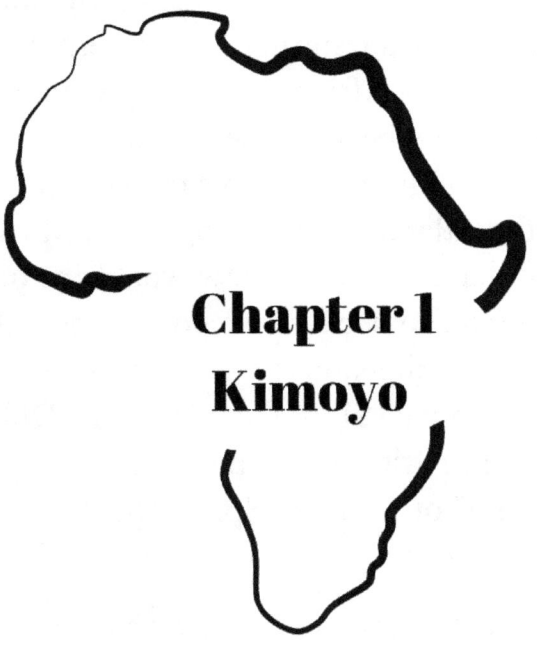

Chapter 1
Kimoyo

When describing the traditions of the many African ethnic groups, we hear the terms African Spirituality, African Traditional Religion, and now the terms Kimoyo which is a better term to describe the traditions of Africa.

Let's talk about the term African Spirituality for a moment. African Spirituality is a term that we, the diaspora Africans, came up with. I understand why because the African Americans were forced to migrate and were displaced during the Atlantic Kidnapping trade. Most of us do not have a clue or know what tribe or clan we belong to, so because we do not know the clan or tribe indigenous religion/spiritual system, we bunch all of them into one. Did we, the diaspora Africans use the word "spirituality" or "African Spirituality" because we rebel against mainstream religion?

In the 21century, we still have a problem with the word religion because of the Western state religion (Christianity, Judaism, and Islam) and how it was used against our Ancestors. I spoke to two continental African brothers, doing the time of me putting together my two-part presentation call African Religion, African Spirituality Concepts, and The How and Why. One of the brothers was from Nigeria and the other from Ghana, and they both told me they use another term to describe the African way of life, and it was African Traditional Religion.

I mention that the diaspora Africans have a problem with the word religion. When the word is mentioned, it triggers so many emotions: anger, hate, sadness, death, enslavement, and the list goes on. In many ways, religions have been defined, so let us look at the discussion from academia and others surrounding the meaning of religion.

The Concepts Of Religion

Etymologically, the term religion lies with the Latin word Religare, which means "to tie, to bind." This seems to be favored on the assumption that it helps explain the power religion has. The Oxford English Dictionary points out, though, that the etymology of the word is doubtful. Earlier writers like Cicero connected the term with relegere, which means "to read over again" (perhaps to emphasize the ritualistic nature of religions).

Austin Cline (2019) What is Religion?

Religion is a set of variously organized beliefs about the relationship between natural and supernatural aspects of reality and the role of humans in this relationship. While religion is difficult to define, one standard model of religion used in religious studies courses was proposed by Clifford Geertz, who simply called it a "cultural system." A critique of Geertz's model by Talal Asad categorized religion as "an anthropological category." Many religions have narratives, symbols, and sacred histories intended to explain the meaning of life and explain the origin of life or the Universe. People derive morality, ethics, religious laws, or a preferred lifestyle from their beliefs about the cosmos and human nature. According to some estimates, there are roughly 4,200 religions in the world (Myovela, 2014: pg. 7).

James (1902), religion is the "feeling, act, and experiences of individual men and women in their solitude, so far as they apprehend themselves to stand in relation to whatever they may consider the divine."

Omoregbe (1999), in his Comparative Religion, defines religion as an interpersonal relationship between a person and a transcendent personal being believed to exist.

To Ekwunife (1990), religion is an awareness and recognition of a dependent relationship on a transcendent Being, the Wholly Other, nameable or un-nameable, personalized or impersonalized expressible in human society through beliefs, worship, and ethical or moral behavior. Just like any other definition of religion, the word 'belief' remains an important core element in the concept of religion. Generally, African people are very religious, and for that matter, religion permeates in all aspects of life, i.e., drumming, dancing, singing, ceremonies, festivals, marriages, among others.

The term "African Traditional Religion" is used in two complementary senses. Loosely, it encompasses all African beliefs and practices that are considered religious but neither Christian nor Islamic. The expression is also used almost as a technical term for a particular reading of such beliefs and practices, one that purports to show that they constitute a systematic whole—a religion comparable to Christianity or any other "world religion."

In that sense, the concept was new and radical when G. Parrinder introduced it in 1954 and later developed by Bolaji Idowu and John Mbiti (see Proponents of African Traditional Religion). These scholars intended to protest against a long history of derogatory evaluations of Africans and their culture by outsiders and to replace words such as "heathenism" and "paganism." African Traditional Religion is now widely taught in African universities, but its identity remains essentially negative.

MacGaffey, Wyatt "African Traditional Religion"

May 06, 2016, https://www.oxfordbibliographies.com/view/docume nt/obo-9780199846733/obo-9780199846733-0064.xml#:~:text=Parrinder%20in%201954%20and%20later,Proponents%20of%20African%20Traditional%20Religion).

Bolaji Idowu

John Mbiti

Geoffrey Parrinder

Kimoyo, this term was introduced to the community by sbA(teacher) Asar Imhotep a year ago. He broke down how anthropologists came into Africa in the early periods and seen these animal representations all across Mother Africa. They were associated with spirit or deities, so in Egypt(Kemet), you see these animals representations of deities with Heru, Anpu, Sutekh, Djehuti, and the list goes on.

Anthropologists use the word animism to reflect the animal representation for the concepts in African Traditional Religion. Most African cultures and traditions believe everything has a spirit; rather, it's animated or inanimated.

Page 115 of K. Fu-Kiau, Self-Healing Power and Therapy (2003) states Moyo, according to ancient schools of Africa, means 'vital power.' Moyo is what is the vitality of life. It is the keyword to Kibantu, the Bantu way of life, their philosophy. Kimoyo ("vitalism") is their religion, and it is not animism.

I want us to look at few pages of K. Fu-Kiau book Self Healing Power and Therapy. He talks about the earth(Futu) and life(Moyo) came into existence so that you can have a little more clarity of Kimoyo, the African religion of vitality. On pages 111-116, Dr. K Fu-Kiau talks about geographers writing what the earth is, and the academic definitions of the earth are not known to the common person inside of Africa. African people do not lack ways to define the planet earth. Their way of defining the planet earth is linked in a very metaphoric way to the essence of life itself. In the eyes of the African people, their teaching of the Earth is futu dia n'kisu diakanga Kalunga mu diambu dai moyo- a sachet (parcel) of medicines tied up by Kalunga for the earth. This futu or funda contains everything life needs for its survival: medicines (n'kisi/bilongo), food (madia), drink (ndwinu), et cetera. Fu-Kiau says futu of medicines consist of chemicals known and unknown by man, which substance exists for one purpose only: Moyo (life) on earth.

Okay, so let us see what K, Fu-Kiau means by the last sentences about the purpose of Moyo (life) on earth. He mentions on page 12 of his book the African approach to the perception of the earth, our planet, as a futu, and it involved six keys, words which are: (1) Futu (sachet, package); (2) n'kisi (medicine); (3) Kanga (to tie, to wrap up) (4) Kalunga (the completely - all-in-all); (5) mudiambu-dia (for); and (6) moyo (life). I will give a brief explanation of the words or terms, and if you want the full explanation or break down, purchase K. Fu-Kiau publications Self-Healing Power and Therapy: Old Teaching From Africa.

Futu

Futu is perceived as the container of something secret and a great price to its owner. It can be made of a piece of cloth, bark, leaf, or animal skin. This charming container and its uses are well-known on the African continent and part of Africa's traditional life. The Futu, if one has to define it, is a container usually made of soft material inside which the owner carries protective or curative medicine, even personal secret objects, such as symbolic objects of secret oaths.

N'kisi

N'kisi of the root-verb kinsa ("to take care") is what takes care of life. The term is synonymous with the word bilongo, "medicine."The n'kisi in this context is always the content of the futu.

Kanga

The word kanga is a verb, "to tie up," usually with a string. Kanga is coding, hiding, neutralizing, preventing, protecting, immunizing as well. When the futu, the container, is filled with the n'kisi, its content, its maker ties it up to hide the secret power of his making.

Kalunga

Kalunga is the one-who-is-complete-by-self, the all-in-all. The term is also used as a synonym and epithet of Nzambi, "God," among the Bantu, especially the

Kongo. Before the introduction of the Judeo-

Christian religion into the area, this term was used to mean the presence of the complete power/energy that gives birth to Moyo (life) and to luyalungunu, universe.

Mu-diambu-dia

These three Kikongo language words together form a compound preposition of intention. They literally mean "in the intention of." This preposition of intention, for, tells us why in what intention this futu dia n'kisi was tied up. For moyo ("life"), it says, according to the teaching, futu, or earth, was made before life appeared in all its forms on earth, well before the existence of plants and animals, including human beings. So everything on and inside the earth, visible or invisible, exists for life and before life.

Moyo

Moyo, the last word in the definition of earth, according to the ancient schools of African, means "vital power." This vital power, Moyo, came to exist on earth after the futu was completely tied up. The futu and its content were ready to secure life to be born on earth.

I like the way K. Fu-Kiau breaks down Moyo further by stating on page 15 Moyo is not luzingu, "the material life." It is not nzingulu, the way this material life is lived or zingu, its duration. All three Luzingu (life), nzingula (living), and zingu (biography) can only be made possible with moyo, the vital power. One who believes in or accepts this notion of vital power is n'kwa-moyo/n'kwa-kimoyo, a vitalist. A vitalist (n'kwa-kimoyo) is an indivdul who believes in the art of regenerating power (dikitisa ngolo/lendo) as the human healing process-dingo-dingo diandiakisina. Moyo is the power that makes things grow and be alive. Moyo as a universal matter is present in everything, even rocks. The kind of Moyo hidden in rocks, plants, and animals has a great role to play in man's moyo and is the main source of medicine.

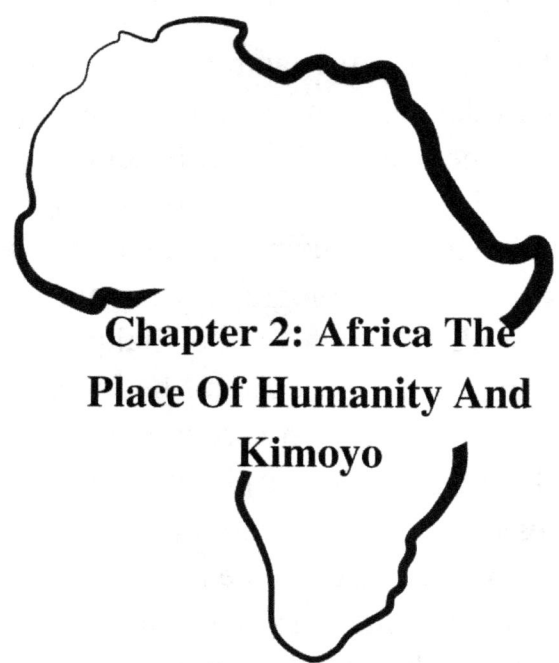

Chapter 2: Africa The Place Of Humanity And Kimoyo

There has been a consensus of Africa being the Mother Continent due to its being the oldest inhabited continent on Earth. Humans and human ancestors have lived in Africa for more than 5 million years. Africa, the second-largest continent, is bounded by the Mediterranean Sea, the Red Sea, the Indian Ocean, and the Atlantic Ocean.

The Rise of Humans (Human Ancestors) Paleoanthropologist Katerina Harvati says anthropologists have discovered thousands of fossils of our extinct ancestors. There is now a pretty good picture of the general pattern of our evolution since the separation of the human lineage from that of the chimpanzees some seven million years ago.

Hominin Timeline

Until recently, it was believed that human evolution was a straightforward process, with a single line species connecting modern humans to an ape-like ancestor. However, our history is much more complicated than this. Many species coexisted and overlapped, and some lineages became extinct along the way. There is no single missing link between our ancestors and those of other apes. Of course, that is not to say we know everything there is to know about human evolution: the fossil record contains only bones that end up in the ideal conditions for preservation. Additionally, the individual members of any species-including modern humans, differ from one another by varying degrees, and different groups separated into distinct species only slowly, through a process of continual change.

(Harvati, Katerina. "The Rise Of Humans." Prehistoric Life, Dorling Kindersley, 2009, pp. 442–479.)

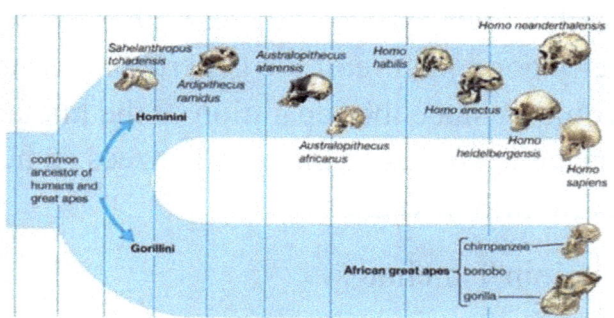

55 million years ago (MYA) First primitive primates evolve.

8 – 6 MYA

First, gorillas evolve. Later, chimp and human lineages diverge.

5.8 MYA

Orrorin tugenensis, the oldest human ancestor thought to have walked on two legs.

5.5 MYA

Ardipithecus, early "proto-human," shares traits with chimps and gorillas and is forest-dwelling.

4 MYA

Australopithecines appear. They have brains no larger than a chimpanzee's – with a volume around 400 – 500 cm3 -, but walk upright on two legs. The first human ancestors to live on the savannah.

3.2 MYA

Lucy, a famous specimen of Australopithecus afarensis, lives near what is now Hadar, Ethiopia.

2.7 MYA

Paranthropus, lives in woods and grasslands, has massive jaws for chewing on roots and vegetation.Becomes extinct 1.2 MYA.

2.5 MYA

Homo habilis appears. Its face protrudes less than earlier hominids but still retains many ape features.

Has a brain volume of around 600 cm3
Hominids start to use stone tools regularly, created by splitting pebbles – this begins the Oldowan tradition of toolmaking, which last a million years. Some hominids develop meat-rich diets as scavengers; the extra energy may have favored the evolution of larger brains.

2 MYA

Evidence of Homo ergaster, with a brain volume of up to 850 cm3, in Africa.

1.8 – 1.5 MYA

Homo erectus is found in Asia. First true huntergatherer ancestor, and also first to have migrated out of Africa in large numbers. It attains a brain size of around 1000 cm3.

1.6 MYA

Possible first sporadic use of fire suggested by discolored sediments in Koobi Fora, Kenya.

More convincing evidence of charred wood and stone tools is found in Israel and dated to 780,000 years ago.

More complex Acheulean stone tools start to be produced and are the dominant technology until 100,000 years ago.

600,000 YA

Homo Heidelbergensis lives in Africa and Europe. Similar brain capacity to modern humans.

500,000 YA

The earliest evidence of purpose-built shelters – wooden huts – are known from sites near Chichibu, Japan.

400,000 YA

Early humans begin to hunt with spears.

325,000 YA

The oldest surviving early human footprints are left by three people who scrambled down the slopes of a volcano in Italy

280,000 YA

First complex stone blades and grinding stones

230,000 YA

Neanderthals appear and are found across Europe, Africa The Place Of Humanity And Kimoyo from Britain in the west to Iran in the east, until they became extinct with the advent of modern humans 28,000 years ago,

195,000 YA

Our species Homo sapiens appears on the scene – and shortly after begins to migrate across Asia and Europe. The oldest modern human remains are two skulls found in Ethiopia that date to this period. The average human brain volume is 1350 cm3 Pickrell, John. "Timeline: Human Evolution." New Scientist, 4 Sept. 2006,(www.newscientist.com/article/dn9989-timelinehuman-evolution/.)

How African Traditional Religion or Kimoyo was founded?

I mention numerous times in presentations and in two publications that some world religions like Judaism, Christianity, and Islam have a founder who started them. This is not the case with African Traditional Religion or Kimoyo. But before I go any further, let us define Judaism, Christianity, and Islam, Judaism is the oldest Abrahamic religion, originating in the people of ancient Israel and Judea.

Judaism is Africa The Place Of Humanity And Kimoyo based primarily on the Torah text, which some Jews believe was handed down to the people of Israel through the prophet Moses. This, along with the rest of the Hebrew Bible and the Talmud, are the central texts of

Judaism. The Jewish people were scattered after the destruction of the Temple in Jerusalem in 70 CE. Today, about 13 million Jews, about 40 percent living in Israel and 40 percent in the United States.

Christianity is based on the life and teachings of Jesus of Nazareth(1st century) presented in the New Testament. The Christian faith is essentially faith in Jesus as the Christ, the Son of God, and as Savior and Lord. Almost all Christians believe in the Trinity, which teaches the unity of Father, Son(Jesus Christ), and Holy Spirit as three persons in one Godhead. Most Christians can describe their faith with the Nicene Creed. As the religion of the Byzantine Empire in the first millennium and of Western Europe during the time of colonization, Christianity has been propagated throughout the world. The main divisions of Christianity are, according to the number of adherents:

•Catholic Church, headed by the Pope in Rome, is a communion of the western church and 22 Eastern Catholic churches.

•Protestantism, separated from the Catholic Church in the 16th-century Reformation and split into many denominations,

•Eastern Christianity, which includes Eastern

Orthodoxy, Oriental Orthodoxy, and the Church of the East. There are other smaller groups, such as Jehovah's Witnesses and the Latter Day Saint movement, whose inclusion in Christianity is sometimes disputed.

Islam is based on the Quran, one of the Holy books considered by Muslims to be revealed by God, and on the teachings of the Islamic prophet Muhammad, a prominent political and religious figure of the 7th century CE. Islam is the most widely practiced religion of Southeast Asia, North Africa, Western Asia, and Central Asia, while Muslim-majority countries also exist in parts of South Asia, Sub-Saharan Africa, and Southeast Europe. There are also several Islamic republics, including Iran, Pakistan, Mauritania, and Afghanistan.

•**Sunni Islamic** the largest denomination within Islam and follows the Quran, the hadiths which record the Sunnah, while placing emphasis on the sahabah.

•**Shia Islamic**, the second-largest denomination of Islam and its adherents, believe that Ali succeeded Prophet Muhammad and further emphasized Prophet Muhammad's family.

•**Ahmadiyyais**, the third-largest denomination of Islam and its adherents, believe that the awaited Imam Mahdi and the Promised Messiah has arrived, believed to be Mirza Ghulam Ahmad by Ahmadis.

Other denominations of Islam include Nation of Islam, Ibadi, Sufism, Quranism, Mahdavia, and non-denominational Muslims. Wahhabism is the dominant Muslim school of thought in the Kingdom of Saudi Arabia.

•**The Baha'i Faith** is an Abrahamic religion founded in the 19th century and has spread worldwide. It teaches the unity of all religious philosophies and accepts all of the prophets of Judaism, Christianity, and Islam as well as additional prophets, including its founder Baha'u'llah.

Smaller regional Abrahamic groups, including Samaritanism(primarily in Israel and the West Bank), the Rastafari movement(primarily in Jamaica), and Druze(primarily in Syria and Lebanon)

African Traditional Religion or Kimoyo evolved slowly through many centuries, as people responded to their life situations and reflected upon their experiences. Many factors must have played a part in its development. These include the geographical environment- mountains, rivers, deserts, and forest the change of the seasons, the powers of nature(such as earthquakes, thunderstorms, and volcanoes), calamities, epidemics, diseases, birth and death, and major historical events like wars, locust invasions, famines, migrations and so on.

So, African's traditional religious or Kimoyo heritage traces its origins to the human quest for meaning and self-understanding. The same question every people have asked themselves and the world in which they live since the dawn of human consciousness how was the world created? How did human and non-human forms of life come to be? Why am I here? What is the meaning of life and death? Our African Ancestors posed these questions, and the answer given to these questions came out of their own unique experiences and reflections. The Answers, pregnant with philosophical and theological meaning, took the form of myths and stories, and these myths and stories would not have come about if people had not asked questions about their existence.

(E. Kofi Agorsah,2010)

Cultural ideas and practices rose and took shape in the process of man's search for answers to these questions and as ways of making human life safer and better. They were influenced by human experience and reflection. No doubt, many of the ideas and practices were later abandoned when they were inadequate.

But, as time went on, these ideas increased in numbers and spread as the people increase dispersed. Many Religious practices sprang up simultaneouslyin different parts of the continent, while others spread through contact among different societies.

Characteristics and Commonalities of African Traditional Religion or Kimoyo

- All things in the universe are part of the whole.There is no sharp distinction between the sacred and the nonsacred.
- In most African traditions, there is a Supreme Being: a creator, sustainer, provider, and controller of all creation.
- Serving with the creator is a variety of lesser and intermediary gods and guardian spirits. These lesser gods are constantly involved in human affairs. People communicate with these gods through rituals, sacrifices, and prayers.
- The human condition is imperfect and always will be. Sickness, suffering, and

death are all fundamental parts of life. Suffering is caused by misdeeds that offend the gods and ancestors or by being out of harmony with society.
- Ritual actions may relieve the problems and sufferings of human life, either by satisfying the offended gods or by resolving social conflicts. Rituals help to restore people to the traditional values and renew their commitment to a spiritual life.

Human society is communal. Ancestors, the living, the living dead, and those yet to be born are essential parts of the community. The relationships between the worldly and the otherworldly help to guide and balance the lives of the community.

Africa The Place Of Humanity And Kimoyo
Humans need to interact with the spirit world, which is all around them. African Traditional Religion or Kimyo differs from religions such as Judaism, Christianity, and Islam. It has no founders like Christ or Muhammad. Kimoyo does not have one hero like those religions that were just named. It has no missionaries or even the desire to propagate the religion or proselytize.

Africans who follow a traditional religion rely on no scriptures, canonical texts, or holy books to guide them. In African traditional religions, guidance is provided through myths, which are handed down orally. Elders, priests, and priestesses have served as guardians of the sacred traditions. Throughout Africa, innumerable myths explain the creation of the universe, how man and woman appeared, the origin of the culture, and how people arrived in their current location. Oral narratives define morals and values for traditional religions, just as written texts do for religions with sacred books.

(Riggs, Thomas. Worldmark Encyclopedia of Religious Practices. Thomson Gale, 2006.)

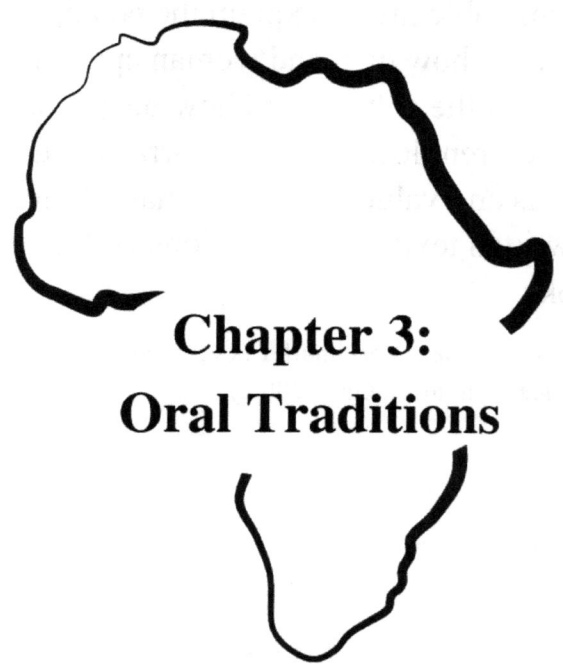

Chapter 3:
Oral Traditions

Over centuries people have formed answers to their questions, often in the form of stories, myths, and proverbs folktales. These answers were passed down by word of mouth from one generation to the next. In this way, oral traditions, many of which address questions of existence from the beginning of time, are established.

(Lugira, Aloysius M. African Traditional Religion. Third ed., Chelsea House, 2009.)

Oral traditions are messages that are transmitted orally and what I like to say from month to ear from generation after generation after generation. These messages were passed down any many ways, such as speech or song, and may take the form of folktales and fables, epic histories and narrations, and proverbs.

J D Fadeiye says oral tradition also includes myths and legends that throw light on community's origin their social, economic, and political institutions, their taboo, totems, social concepts, and practices.

(Fadeiye, J, D.(2004). Historiography and Methods of Teaching History for N.C.E and Undergraduates. Oyo)

Many uninformed people say oral traditions is not a reliable source, but yes, oral traditions is a reliable source because African non-writing societies use the oral method of oral tradition to convey their custom, history, traditions, folklore, myths, saying from generation to generation. Many lean on writing as more reliable than orally, and those who make that statement are too lazy to read and studied African oral traditions. By the way, writing relies on oral traditions, but oral traditions don't rely on writing. There are many ways of oral traditions, so let us look at three main categories of oral traditions.

African oral tradition has three main categories

1. Literary

2. Historical

3. Erudite

• "The literary" includes poetic genres, divination

poems, and songs. It also includes proverbs, parables,

and incantations.

• "The historical" includes narratives based on

myths, legends, and historical plays or epics.

• "The erudite" category encompasses secrets

formulas, prayers, and any corpus of an esoteric nature.

Griot and Griotte

The Griots has many roles such as Poet, Historian, Advisors, Spokesperson, Peacemakers, Diplomats, Praise-singers, Interpreters, Translators, Musicians, Composers, Teachers, Warriors and Storyteller.

"The oral skill of the poet, Africans recognize their orature and its performance (one cannot have one without the other) as a functional part of society. The purpose of orature is not merely to entertain or appeal to emotions or physical senses but also to enlighten and stir the audience into some productive action or initiate or facilitate spiritual action.

African orature does not departmentalize literature into poetry, prose, and drama, but just language used by the speaker or poet. Examples of the use of language rooted in indigenous African culture are copious. This is important because it demonstrates no line drawn between a speech act and a performance in African communities. They are the same. To speak is to perform. Traditional African literature, or

African orature, exists alongside or within African languages."

(Finnegan, Ruth H. Oral Literature in Africa. Oxford Univ. Press, 1993.)

WEST AFRICAN FABLES & FOLKTALES

West African fables & folktales are full of wisdom and generally convey a moral or teach a lesson. Often these lessons are ones of resourcefulness, independence and illustrate the rewards of courage. There are different types of folktales, with fables and talking beasts' stories among the most common.

Many of Africa's oral tales are types such as

- Traditional Hunting Song

- Trickster Tale

- Dilemma Tale

- Chain Tale

In Aloysius M. Lugira's third editions of his book, African Traditional Religion, he states "stories," and fables usually illustrate some truth about human nature and end with a stated or unstated moral. Such stories are partly for entertainment, but they are more than just amusing tales. They are the African way of teaching and passing down ethics, or correct behavior, to the next generation. One of the most famous African folk heroes is Anansi, the spider. Anansi is the hero of many folktales of the Akan people of West Africa.

The Anansi tales have crossed from West Africa to the Americas, where they are familiar to many children. Anansi is a trickster. Tricksters may be human or animal or a little of both, but they all have superhuman powers to use for good or for harm. They also suffer from many of the character flaws that ordinary humans have, such as greed and envy. As a result, they are often caught in their own snares. Stories about Anansi, or as he is usually called, Father Anansi, attribute great skill and ingenuity. In one tale, Anansi tries to take back the wisdom he has distributed in the world by storing it in a large pot. However, when he is challenged by his son Ntikuma, Anansi angrily allows the pot to fall from the top of a tree, and human beings can gather it up for themselves.

(Asihene, Emmanuel V. Traditional Folk-Tales of Ghana. Edwin Mellen Press, 1997.)

Storytelling

"There is a rich tradition throughout Africa about oral storytelling. Although written history existed for centuries in West Africa, most writings were in Arabic, and most people did not read or write in Arabic. So the transmission of knowledge, history, and experience in West Africa was mainly through oral tradition and performance rather than written texts.

Oral traditions guide social and human morals, giving people a sense of place and purpose. There is often a lesson or a value to instill, and the transmission of wisdom to children is a community responsibility. Parents, grandparents, and relatives take part in passing down the knowledge of culture and history. Storytelling provides entertainment, develops the imagination, and teaches important lessons about everyday life."

(World Affairs Council of Houston."The Oral Traditions of Africa." Teach African, static1.squarespace.com/static/53cfd0e5e4b057663ea1bc61/t/57b1e0b746c3c406dd172afd/1471275383444/Oral+Traditions+of+West+Africa.pdf.)

"A storyteller's tools are not just words, but gestures, singing, facial expressions, body movements, and acting to make stories memorable and interesting. Sometimes masks and costumes are used to enhance a performance. A storyteller performs epics that can be hours or even days long that relate history and genealogy, battles, and political uprisings of a community. They use riddles, proverbs, and myths to educate and entertain. Storytelling is an important shared event with people sitting together, listening, and even participating in accounts of past deeds, beliefs, taboos, and myths."

I have argued that performance arts started in Africa; Africa storytelling is a performance art that creates bonds among community members and transmits traditional culture values, history, war victories, past events, etc.

Creations Myths

From human's earliest beginnings, African people have asked questions about their existence, which was mention in chapter 2. Their questions such as, Who are we? How did we come to be here? How should we understand our place in this world? These questions have given rise to the rich and varied creation myths of African peoples.

Myths of creation tell of the sacred beginnings of the people. They usually center on a Supreme Being who, according to African oral tradition, created the world. They recognize the special position the Creator has given to humankind. African Creation myths often tell about the special relationship between the Supreme Being and the first people. The human being is imperfect, made mistakes for which they must be punished. One example the Dinka people say is that once a rope hung down from heaven, people could climb up when they wanted to talk to their God. But an older woman mashing yams kept hitting the underside of heaven with her pestle, and weary of the noise, the God pulled up the rope and withdrew the heavens to a higher plane. Still, people are always encouraged to make up for their failures. African myths commonly conclude with a lesson about the importance of people living well in this world.

Heroes

(Lugira M. Aloysius 2009) Human life is generally marked by success and failure and a variety of minor ups and downs. Hero tales and legends focus on success, encouraging a positive group image. In African traditions, many heroes are human beings who are deified, that is, elevated to the status of gods. Through their acts on Earth, they become associates of the Supreme Being. A hero maybe someone who does a great deed for the community or someone who seems touched by the gods, specially chosen from childhood for some higher purpose.

Shango is one in the Yoruba culture in Nigeria, who was a hero, and who was eventually deified. Imhotep in Egypt(Kemet) also was a hero who was also deified after death. Shango and Imhotep are very popular stories but let us talk about Lubaale Muska of Baganda people in Uganda. This hero story may not be popular or familiar to some, but Lubaale Muskaa, a god of the Baganda people, who was a deified hero, a human who has become a god.

(The title Lubaale refers to a spiritual being.) When, as a child, he disappeared from his home and appeared mysteriously on another island, the people there thought he must be superhuman to have appeared, seemingly out of nowhere. He refused to eat anything but the heart and liver of an ox, and he drank its blood, confirming the people's opinion that he was a god. The people soon began consulting him on matters of health and money. When he disappeared as mysteriously as he had arrived,

Lubaale Mukasa was acknowledged as one of the highest-ranking gods of their people.

The oral traditions constitute the method of transmitting the history and traditions by spoken rather than written means. Oral Traditions make it possible for a society to pass knowledge across generations without writing. They help people make sense of the world and teach children and adults about important aspects of their culture.

Chapter 4: Supreme Deities and Lesser Deities

Name of the Supreme Being
Central African Regions

Country	Ethnicity	Name	Meaning
Burundi	Barundi	Imana	The Creator of everything
Cameroon	Bumum Bulu Duala	Njinyi Mabee Ebasi	He who is everywhere, He who sees and hears everything. The one who bears the world Omnipotent father
Central African republic	Baya	Zambi	Creator
Congo Vili (Brazzaville)	Vili	Nzambi	Creator and ultimate
Congo (Kinshasa)	Baluba	Vidye	Great creator Spirit
Gabon	Fang	Mebe'e	Creator
Rwanda	Banyarwanda	Imana	The Creator of everything
Zambia	Ambo Barotse, Baila	Leza Nyambi	Creator Creator

Supreme Deities and Lesser Deities

Eastern African Regions

Country	Ethnicity	Name	Meaning
Kenya	Akamba	Mumbi	Creator, Maker, Fashioner
Sudan	Nuer / Dinka, Shilluk	Kwoth / Jok, Juok	Creator Spirit / Creator Spirit
Tanzania	Chagga, Gogo Nyakyusa, Bazinza	Ruwa Mulungu Kyala Kazooba	Sun Creator Owner Of Allthing Power of the Sun
Uganda	Baganda, Alur Banyankore	Katonda, Jok Ruhanga	Creator Originator Creator Spirit Creator and Fixer of Everything

Supreme Deities and Lesser Deities

Western African Regions

Country	Ethnicity	Name	Meaning
Benin	Fon	Nana-Buluku Mawu-lisa	Original Creator Continuer of creation
Burkina Faso	Tallensi	Wene	Sky God
Senegambia	Serer	Rog	Creator
Ghana	Akan, Ashanti	Nyame	The Shining One
Nigeria igbo	Igbo Yoruba	Chwuku Olodumare	Great Spirit The Most Supreme Being
Sierra Leone	Mende Kono	Leve Yataa	The High-Up one The one you meet everywhere

Supreme Deities and Lesser Deities

Southern African Regions

Country	Ethnicity	Name	Meaning
Angola	Bakongo Ovimbundu	Nzambi Suku	Creator He who supplies the needs of His creatures
Botswana	Tswana	Modimo	The Great Spirit
Lesotho	Basuto	Molimo	The Great Spirit
Malawi	Chewa Ngoni	Mulungu Uluhlanga	The Creator The original Source
South Africa	Zulu	Unkulunkulu	The Oldest One
Swaziland	Swazi	Mvelamqandi	"Who-appeared-first," the power above, unapproachable, unpredictable, of no specific sex
Zimbabwe	Shona Ndebele	Mwari Unkulunkulu	He who is in, or owns the sky, the great one of the Sky, The great oldest one

At the bottom is a small chart of a few of the lesser deities but first, let me explain what lesser deities are in my own words.

The supreme being created the lesser deities, and the lesser deities are under the Supreme Being. They are a link between the people and the supreme being. The lesser deities facilitate many roles and jobs. They are in various departments of life, and they are also involved in the day-to-day activities of humans; they answer prayers, send messages, etc.

Country	Ethnicity	Name
Nigeria	Igbo	Alusi
Ghana	Akan	Abosom
Senegal	Serer	Pangool
Benin, Togo	Fon	Vodun
Nigeria	Yoruba	Orisha
Egypt	Remetch	Netcherew

African cosmogonic narratives explain how the world was put into place by a divine personality, usually the Supreme God, in collaboration with lesser supernatural beings who act on his behalf or aid in the creative process. In several cultures, a supreme deity performs creation through mere thought processes. In other cases, the Supreme Being instructs lesser deities on how to create by providing them with materials to undertake uninhabited by animate beings. In African cosmological narratives, creation is always portrayed as a complex process, whether the universe has evolved from preexisting matter or divine thought.

(Zvawanda , Stephen.African Traditional Religions.)

Serer Mythology (Creation story)

The creation myth of the Serer people is intricately linked to the first trees created on Planet Earth by Roog. Earth's formation began with a swamp. The Earth was not formed until long after the creation of the first three worlds: the waters of the underworld, the air, which included the higher world (i.e., the sun, the moon, and the stars), and the earth. Roog is the creator and fashioner of the Universe and everything in it. The creation is based on a mythical cosmic egg and the principles of chaos.

First Human According to the Serer Before humans existed, there were three stages in the creation of the Universe, and each of these steps followed a consistent order. The first phase was the first three elements: air, earth, and water. The mythical words of Roog found in a nax led to the formation of the heavens, earth, and the sea. The second phase of the creation was the primordial trees (i.e., Somb, Nqaul, Nquf, etc.,). The third phase was the creation of the animal world: the jackal and "Mbocor" (which means "The Mother) - mother of all animals except the jackal. In each of these phases, and before the creation of the first human couple, the supreme deity did not directly create each species but only the primogenitors. They then went on to populate the world with all the species of plant and animal life.

The same was the case at the creation of the first humans. By thought, the supreme deity planned to create human beings (a female and a male). By words, Roog went through a gestation phase that signaled man and woman's gestation, paired within divine placenta. Through its maternal nature, Roog projected a female and male human being as in childbirth. The first human was a female named YAAB. The second human was a male named YOP(var: YOB).

YAAB and YOP were the first humans that walked the Earth, according to the narrative. The ancient and sacred village of Yaabo-Yabo (var: Yaboyabo or YABO-YABO, in present-day Senegal) also derives its name from this couple.

(Sundara, Oscar. Serer Religion. Duc, 2012.)

Zulu Mythology (Creation Story)

At first, there was nothing but darkness. Earth was a lifeless rock. But in that darkness dwelt a god, Umvelinqangi, whose voice was like thunder and who, when angered, would shake the world with earthquakes. Umvelinqangi created a single tiny seed. He sent it to the Earth. This seed was the very first life, from which all other life descended. It landed in the soil and sprouted into a long reed. The reed dropped more seeds, which fell off and grew into even more reeds. This continued until they covered a massive swamp to the north, the land called Uthlanga. At the end of one reed, there grew a man. His name was Unkulunkulu, known as "the first ancestor" and "the Great

One." Very small at first, he grew so large and heavy that he snapped off the end of the reed. Walking across the land of Uthlanga, he noticed men and women were sprouting at the ends of the other reeds. He picked them from the reeds. These people were the first humans, the ancestors of all nations, and they spread across the Earth. It was from Uthlanga that the ancestors of the Zulu journeyed south to the fertile lands they inhabit today.

The Great One continued to walk among the reeds. He saw many forms of life growing at the end of them. He gathered the fish and flung them into the rivers. Fields and forests began to grow, so he harvested birds and antelope, and they darted off into the wild. He picked cattle so humans could use them. He plucked off a ball of fire and a round glowing stone and flung them into the sky. These were the Sun and Moon. The light came into the world.

The Great One also plucked from the reeds fierce lions and other beasts that would travel the lands hunting prey. He harvested magical creatures, some good and some bad. One was the snake-like goddess of the rivers, Mamlambo, rumored by some Zulu to drown people, eat their faces, and suck out their brains. Another goddess was Mbaba Mwana Waresa, a beautiful woman who created rain and rainbows, invented farming, and gave the Zulu the gift of beer.

One of the final acts of the Great One was the most tragic. He plucked the first chameleon off a reed and sent it to give humans the following message: "Men must not die." By the words of the Great One, humans would become immortal. Unfortunately, the chameleon was slow and lazy in his journey. The Great One grew impatient and picked a different lizard from a reed.

This lizard was fast and quickly arrived to give the word to the humans. But the lizard did not bear the exact instructions. Instead, the lizard uttered the words, "Men must die." And so, from that day, humans became mortal. It is said that chameleons change color because they are so ashamed their ancestor was not fast enough to spare humankind the invention of death.

(Lynch, Patricia Ann, and Jeremy Roberts. African Mythology: A to Z. 2nd ed. New York: Chelsea House, 2010.)

Fon Mythology (Creations Story)

Nana Buluku, an androgynous supreme God. From Nana Buluku came the twin deities, Mawu and Lisa. Mawu-Lisa(also spelled Mahu-Lisa, Mahou-Lissa, or Mahu-Lissa) is the first on the list of primary deities in the Dahomean Vodun pantheon. Mawu and Lisa (also called Segbo-Lisa) are the creators couple of Heaven and Earth. Mawu, the female principle, corresponds to the moon and is associated with night, fertility, motherhood, gentleness, forgiveness, rest, and joy, all characteristics that one sees in women. Lisa, the male principle, corresponds to the sun and is associated with day, heat, work, power, war, strength, toughness, and intransigence, all things that characterize men.

They are xoxo, 'twins,' and their union is regarded as the basis of the universal order. It is a concept that has parallels elsewhere. In Chinese mythology, the primordial woman, T'ai Yuan, sometimes combined the masculine Yang and the feminine Yin in her person—the two interacting forces that sustain the cosmos. Likewise, among the Zuni Indians of North America, Awonawilona, the creator and sustainer of the world, is he-she.

Fon cosmology envisages the earth as floating on water, the source of rain, and the springs beneath the surface of the ground. Above the earth, circle the heavenly bodies on the inner surface of a gourd. Serpentine power, personified as Da, son of the divine pair, assists in ordering this cosmos. A serpent has a dual nature rather than a female-male identity. When he appears in the rainbow, 'the male is the red portion, the female the blue.' Above the earth, Da has 3,500 coils, xasa-xasa, and the same number below together, they support Mawu-Lisa's creation. A way of describing this cosmic interrelationship would be to say that Mawu-Lisa is thought and Da is action. Other voduns, of course, are assigned parts in the government of the world. Now let us discuss the seven most essential Voduns in Fon traditions and see their role or job. I will discuss one more pantheon in full detail, but the last two pantheons Ill give the names only.

Pantheon

Voduns

· Sakpata: This is the eldest son of Mawu to whom the earth was entrusted: "Ayi Vodun," the Vodun of the earth. His power is feared and terrifying. His attributes are the arm of

69

smallpox, scissors, a chain, and black, white, and red spots. Sakpata has many sons, including the Vodun of leprosy (Ada Tangni) and incurable sores (sinji aglosumato).

· Xêvioso (or Xêbioso): This is the Vodun of the sky (Jivodun) who manifests himself in thunder and lightning. He is Mawu's second son and is considered a Vodun of justice who punishes thieves, liars, criminals, and evil-doers. His attributes are the thunderbolt, the double ax, the ram, the color red, and fire. Xêvioso has several sons including Sogbo, Aklobè, Avlékété.

· Agbe: This is the Vodun of the sea (Tovodun). He is also known as Hu. He is represented by a serpent, a symbol of everything that gives life. One of his powerful children is Dan Toxosu, who manifests himself in the birth of monster babies.

· Gu: This is the Vodun of iron and war. He gives man his different technologies. He is the Vodun who does not accept complicity with evil. Therefore he is capable of killing all accomplices in acts of infamy if he is appealed to. This is expressed by the Fon saying, "da gu do".

- Agê: This fifth son of Mawu is the Vodun of agriculture and the forests. He reigns over animals and birds.

- Jo: This Vodun is characterized by invisibility. He is the Vodun of the air.

- Lêgba: This is Mawu's youngest son. He received no endowments at all because all had already been shared out among his elders. He is jealous, and it is he who loosens the rigid structure of the pantheon. He is the Vodun of the unpredictable, of what cannot be assigned to any other, and daily tragedies characterize him; all that is beyond good and evil.

Lubaale

- Ggulu Literally, Ggulu means "sky," "heaven." It is the name both of heaven and the sky deity. Ggulu is thus the divinity next to Katonda, the Supreme Being.

In Buganda lore, the wife of the founder of the Buganda kingdom was the daughter of Ggulu, who came to Earth from heaven with her brother Walumbe. The Buganda people originate with her, and therefore from heaven.

- Kiwanuka

Kiwanuka means "something that descends at a great speed." Kiwanuka is a deity of thunder and lightning. He is also a god of fertility whom couples consult when they wish to have a child. When their prayers are successful, parents often name their child for the god: Kiwanuka for a son or Nakiwanuka for a daughter.

- Kita ka

Kitaka is believed to be Mother Earth. The king consulted this divinity in cases of capital punishment so that the spirits of the dead would not return to harm him. People also consult Kitaka bout cultivating the land to have abundant crops.

- Wa lumbe

The literal translation of this god's name is "Mr. Death." Walumbe is the son of Ggulu, the sky deity, and the brother-in-law of Kintu, the first king of Buganda. When Walumbe's sister, the king's wife, made the mistake of forgetting to bring some provisions to Earth and went back to the sky to fetch them, Walumbe, her brother, returned to Earth with her. Since then, Mr. Death has lived in the underworld as the divinity of death. A temple to him, built and cared for at Tanda in Uganda, reminds the population of the existence of death.

Wanga

Wanga is one of the oldest of the population of the deified heroes of the Baganda. These "terrestrial gods," lower ranking than the "sky deities" who rule in heaven, are the ones to whom the Baganda turn on daily with their prayers and concerns. In the traditions of the Baganda people, the Sun once fell from the sky. The king called upon Wanga. He rose to the challenge and restored the Sun in its place in the heavens. As a reward, the king allotted an estate to Wanga and built a temple there. People consult Wanga about sickness and disease. He also foretells how people may turn aside calamities and troubles that befall communities.

Musisi

Musisi is the son of Wanga. His name means "earthquake." The Baganda people turn to him during natural calamities such as earthquakes.

Mukasa

Mukasa is a deified hero of the Baganda. Of all the superhuman beings within the Lubaale who invisibly populate the Earth and are in daily contact with humans, he ranks highest. People turn to Mukasa with concerns for health and fertility.

Kibuuka

Kibuuka, the brother of Mukasa, is the war god of the Baganda. Consultation regarding warfare and national defense is directed to him, together with his nephew Nende, also a divinity of war.

Alusi

· Ala

· Ikenga

· Igwe

· Anyanwu

· Agwu

· Ahia Njoku

· Amadioha

· Ekwensu

· Aro

· Njoku Ji

· Ogbunabali

Orisha

· Obatala

· Ogun

· Oshun

· Oya

· Shango

· Yemoja

· Eshu

In this chapter, we learn that it is an explanation that describes the beginning of humanity, earth, life, and the universe in most African cosmogonies. The supreme deity carries out creation and has a pantheon of minor or lesser deities, which helps the supreme being by aiding it in its creations. There are tons of African creations story in all of Africa. I couldn't mention all of them in this one chapter, but maybe I can make that a project in the future by putting out a publication of all the African Creation myths.

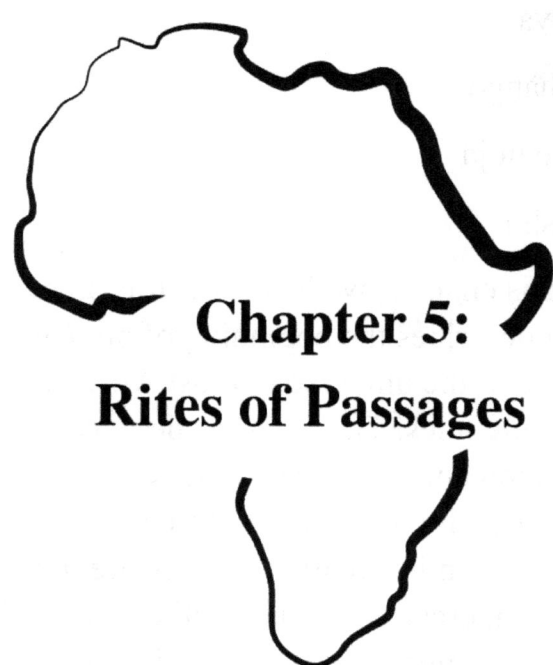

Chapter 5:
Rites of Passages

According to Denise Martin, Rites of Passages is one's journey through life, carrying out a particular destiny and asserting one's humanity; one should become complete and perfect. This perfection, in turn, allows a person to become an ancestor, which is the ultimate purpose of life. Through rites of passage, set up by the community, people undergo a series of transformative processes that will assist them in their development as human beings. Rites of passage have played a significant role in African communities for hundreds of years. They are well-thought-out and effective programs designed to allow people to move with little stress to the next phase of their existence.

I agree with what Denise Martin said about the African Rites of passages. I always explain the rite passages to our subscribers on YouTube as a central role in African socialization, demarking the different stages in an individual's development and that person's relationship and role to the broader community.

In each rite, you must be initiated, and the African initiation rites are stated as the fundamentals of human growth and development. These rites "Birth," "Adulthood," "Circumcision," "Marriage," "Eldership,"

"Ancestor," Death," and in some other ethnic groups, "Scarification and "Piercing" were originally established by our African ancestors while they were living to link the individual to the community.

Birth/Name Rite

The rite of birth is the first major rite. Nearly all African cultures believe that the infant has come from the spirit world with important information from that world and brings unique talents and gifts; indeed, a unique purpose, mission, message, or project to offer to the community and thus a reason for celebration. Therefore, the Rite of Birth is the first of the major rites and involves initiating the infant into the world through a ritual and naming ceremony. It is the responsibility of the family and community to discover through consultation with elders and diviners to determine this mission. This can be accomplished through rituals, birth charts, etc. It is important to clearly determine the new community member's mission in order to successfully guide him/her along their life path. The naming of the infant is seen as an essential part of the birthing rite, as it is believed that names have a spiritual vibration that affects the person as an infant, into adult life, and beyond.

(Davis, Tasha. "African Rites of Passage." African Holocaust Society, April 24. 2017, africanholocaust.net/ritesofpassage/.)

Before I get into the naming ceremony, I just wanted to highlight that the child does not exist until they get their name. The naming ceremony may take place on different days in different societies in Africa. Also, in some cultures, girls are name first, and boys name a few days after, i.e. girls name in 7 days after birth and boys 14 days after birth, but generally, a child is named within 7 to 9 days of birth. If we look at the Yoruba and Akan people, a child is usually named on the 8th day. At the naming ritual, the child receives between 2 and 30 names depending on the occasion and birth.

Name Customs/Rite

Kimoyo is expressed in the names of people and places. Most African names of people and places have symbolic meanings that are religious in nature. Names are chosen for their special meaning, power, and source. Names are often circumstantial, and historical narratives are woven around them. Newborns are named based on specific situations surrounding their birth, and the names may be related to the feeling of the parents, time of birth, description of the child, or his or her background. Naming a child is taken seriously because it is believed that a name can make a person.

I am an African American born in Mississippi. Once I became aware or conscious, as some would say, I began to study ancient Egyptian history and then, later, multiple West African groups. After noticing that African names were important and meant something, I took on the name of the Akan People of Ghana.

The Akan name their children after the days of the week in the order in which they were born. I was born on a Friday morning, and I am my mother's firstborn child out of her four children, so my name is Kofi Piesie. Kofi means born on Friday, and Piesie means firstborn.

In many societies, the naming ritual is enacted during the early hours of the day. The seventh or eighth day marks a transition and a complete departure from the spirit world to the world of the living. It is a rite usually carried out within the family compound, and participation is limited, although not strictly restricted to relatives and the extended family. An elder or a renowned personality in the family conducts the ritual in the presence of both maternal and paternal family relatives seated outside in the family compound.

The naming ritual is also accompanied by the presentation of money and gifts, which symbolically represent objects to commence the life journey. Pouring of libations is poured to venerate and invoke the blessing of the family Ancestors on behalf of the newborn baby.

Initiation

Professor and anthropologist Mwalimu J. Shujaa states initiation is a process of cultural transmission and community survival. It is always a collective responsibility. Nearly all African cultural groups mark significant points of transition throughout the life cycle by rituals and ceremonies related to birth, end of childhood, and beginning of adult life, marriage, eldership, and death.Generally, African cosmogonies view the human life span as a journey along a spiraling cycle in which the individual exists in the spirit world before birth, is embodied and born into the physical world, and, at death, the disembodied spirit returns to the spirit world to be reborn in physical form.

Rite of Adulthood

The Rite of Adulthood is the second major initiation rite, and it is nowadays the most popular among the set of rites. Most people today assume that "rites of passage" only refers to initiation into adulthood. They are often not aware that adulthood rites are only one set of rites within a larger system of rites. Adulthood rites are usually done at the onset of puberty age (around 12-13 years of age in many cultures). They are to ensure the shaping of productive, community-oriented responsible adults. There is nothing automatic about youth being productive members of society, nor is there anything complicated about transitioning from a child to an adult.

(Davis, Tasha. "African Rites of Passage." African Holocaust Society, April 24. 2017, africanholocaust.net/ritesofpassage/.)

Children are taught the necessary skills for adulthood. This includes problem-solving, rules and taboos of society, social responsibility, what is considered appropriate behavior for women and men, and instructions in matters of sexual life, marriage, procreation, family responsibilities, and their purpose or life mission. These are something the children are learning in isolation from the community, which prepares them to be adults if they meet suitable proficiencies in these lessons. Now there are other levels in the adulthood rite. Some are initiated in the rite at 14, 16, or order. When he or she reaches thirty years of age, one is prepared for senior adulthood; when he or she is in their fifties, one is being prepared for the junior elder role. Eldership is between sixty and seventy-five, but we will touch on this rite little later in this chapter. The completion and success of the rite of adulthood are publically celebrated with a "coming out ceremony" or reintroduction to society. The young girls and boys are now celebrated as adults with their families and the there community. There is a lot of good food, singing, dancing by the community, and performances by the newly initiated adults.

I like to give one example of the Karo and Hamar people of the Omo Valley adult rites passages. The Karo, like the Hamar, perform the Bula or Pilla initiation rite, which signifies the coming of age for young men. The initiate must demonstrate that he is ready to "become a man" by leaping over rows of cattle six times consecutively without falling. If successful, the boy will become eligible for marriage (as long as his older brothers are already married). He will be allowed to appear publicly with the elders in sacred areas.

Marriage

The Rite of Marriage represents the joining of two families and even communities; it also represents the joining of the two missions of the new couple. This means that in addition to performing marriage rites for the coming together of male and female, for the purpose to procreate, perpetuate life, and join families. It is also an institution to help the husband and wife to fulfill their mission and objectives in life, ensuring that they are working together towards the same end. A very high value is placed on marriage in African society. Because the focus is on the collective, it is not uncommon that full social standing and adulthood can only be achieved by marriage. In some societies, marriage is not recognized fully until the wife gives birth.

(Asante, Molefi Kete, and Ama Mazama. Encyclopedia of African Religion. SAGE, 2009.)

I have said this time and time again, children are an asset to their family and community. The marriage rite is the most critical rite out of them all. Thus, to thoroughly grasp the significance of marriage in Kimoyo and life, one must fully understand the meaning of childbearing for African people. The preservation and transmission of life is the highest African cultural value. The birth of many children is consequently seen as a blessing because those children will ensure the continuation and strengthening of the family lineage and the community at large. Also, the children will be responsible for ensuring that their parents receive proper burial rites and for performing commemorative rituals that, in turn, will maintain the deceased in a state of immortality through their continued connection with the world of the living.

Eldership

The Rite of Eldership is the fourth major initiation rite, and it is an important component of the initiation system because it is the elders who represent tradition and the wisdom of the past. In African culture, there is a fundamental distinction that has to be made between an "elder" and "older" person.

An older person has simply lived a longer life than most people, but it is not considered one who deserves high praise and respect. This is because the older person's life has not been a positive example for the community. An older person could be a thief or drunkard, an evil person, or could be someone who never married and had children. Thus these examples would undoubtedly prevent a person from being considered a respected elder.

On the other hand, an elder is given the highest status in African culture because she/he has lived a life of purpose, and there is nothing more respected than living a purposeful life. The life of an elder is centered in the best tradition of the community. An elder has gone through all of the previous three rites and is a living model for the other groups in the society to emulate. An elder is given the highest status and along with new infants because these two groups represent the closest links to the wisdom of the spirit world.

To become an elder, one must pass through all rites of passage from birth to old age, i.e., birth rite, adulthood rite, circumcision rite, marriage rite, elder or eldership Rite, ancestor/death rite.

What is an Elder?

Elders are the guardians of the culture, traditions, and history of the people. Integrity, generosity, wisdom, articulateness, subtlety, patience, tactfulness, gratefulness, and being listened to and respected by others are all qualities of an Elder. Understandably, with Eldership, one's status and value in the community rise.

What are the roles of an elder?

The primary work of the Elder is to advise, guide, and oversee the living in the community; their fundamental value and purpose lies in teaching the young what it means to be human. The Elder knows the traditions, history, values, beliefs, and cultural laws that are inviolate. Accordingly, the experience and wisdom of the Elder are readily sought and freely shared with others. Elders are charged with the task of understanding both the material and spiritual requisites of life. It is thought to be an honor to even be in the presence of an Elder. They serve as a link between the past and the present while guaranteeing that our way of life is extended into the future.

("Elders ." Encyclopedia of African Religion, by Wade W. Nobles, SAGE, 2009, pp. 236 23.)

Further Roles of Elders in African Communities

(1) They fix dates for community rituals and ceremonies.

(2) They advise the members of the community on what steps to take during times of difficulties.

(3) They make major decisions affecting families and the community.

(4) They settle disputes in the community.

(5) They give instructions and guidelines on various issues.

(6) They teach the youth on their responsibilities and the general customs of the community.

(7) They negotiate for peace with others.

(8) Occasionally they preside over worship practices.

(9) They are the custodians of traditions and customs of the community.

(10) They preside over the distribution of property.

(11) Preside over religious ceremonies

(12) Judging cases.

(13) Punishing/ fining the offenders.

(14) Praying for the community.

(15) Overseeing the sharing of community wealth/property etc.

(16) Mediating between God and people/ancestors/spirits.

(17) Advises and guides the community.

(18) Formulating laws governing the community/ensuring laws are kept

(19) Facilitating reconciliation

What are Ancestors?

Ancestors are those who once lived in human society and, having fulfilled certain conditions, are now in the realm of the spirits. One becomes an ancestor by living and dying in a particular way. In Kimoyo, to become an ancestor, one must have lived an exemplary life, shown devotion to one's ancestors respected the elders, and had children. Among various ethnic groups, to become an ancestor, one must have died a good death; that is, one's death must not have been by suicide, accident, or other forms of violence, with the possible exception of heroic deaths on the battlefield. In most societies, those dying of epilepsy, leprosy, and lunacy cannot be considered candidates for ancestor -hood.

So we see a notable difference between an older person who dies and is seen as nothing more than a dead relative; without honor, and will not be remembered as a great person, nor is someone who should be followed or emulated. A respected elder who passes is a revered and respected ancestor given the highest honor. This group of ancestors wields excellent power and is often called upon in matters of trouble or uncertainty to help influence a favorable outcome. Ancestors are respected elders who have passed away and continue to serve as an extension of the family and community.

Ancestorship/Death

The final of the initiation rites concerns the soul passing into another continuous phase of existence, the spirit world. It is an extension of the elder distinction because a person's status in life is the same status that they bring with them when they pass on. In African societies, there is little distinction between the sacred and the secular. The spirit is a part of the All, and therefore when a person dies, it is believed that communication and ties with the living continues. Because African philosophy from one culture to another agrees that the deceased's spirit is still with the living community, a distinction must be made in the status of the various spirits, as there are distinctions made in the status of the living.

(Prof. Manu Ampim 2003)

Funeral

The funeral and birth and marriage are a major life ceremony in many African cultures because it encompasses the full transmission of life. The numerous rituals associated with the preparation and placement of the body, mourning, securing the destiny of the deceased, establishing a new relationship with the deceased, and restoring communal relationships reflect an affirmation of the continuity of life. There are variations in funeral rites according to the deceased's age, marital status, and community standing.

"Circumcision," "Scarification," and **"Piercing** are rites that I didn't discuss, and these rites are not practiced across the board in Africa, but the Circumcision rite is a little controversial when it comes to women, which have now been banned in many African societies. Scarification is a long and painful process and a permanent modification of the body, transmitting complex messages about identity and social status. Permanent body markings emphasize social, political, and religious roles. It was also performed on girls to mark stages of life: puberty, marriage, etc. Facial scarification in West Africa was used to identify ethnic groups, families, individuals and express beauty; scars were thought to beautify the body. In African societies, piercing of the ears, lips, and nose and stretching with objects such as straw, wood, plates, and even bones is a part of initiation into adulthood and preparation for marriage.

I think if we start to implement our Rites of Passages that we forgot via slave trade back into the Homes, Communities, Cities, States, we would have long-lasting marriages, fewer people barring kids without marriage. More people knowing their gifts and purpose in life and sharing it. More men and not men still being boys, more elders, and less older. More women being women and describing themselves as Queens and not as B__ches and H_ers. More men describing themselves as Kings and not N___ers. More respect for our communities and better neighbors. More reverence and praises to those who came before us, such as our Ancestors who have transitioned into the invisible or spiritual realm. I can keep going, but you get the picture.

With all that said, suppose we were to decide in the future as a community to put these rites of passages into practice for the betterment of our behaviors and the overall betterment of our families and communities. Yes, we definitely would have to update and modify each rite to fit our standards in this new day.

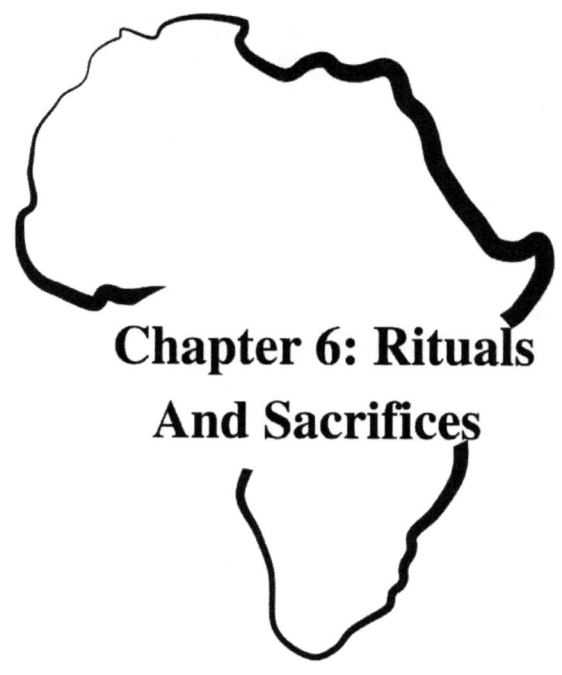

Chapter 6: Rituals And Sacrifices

Ritual

A ritual is a sequence of activities involving gestures, words, actions, or objects, performed in appropriate circumstances, in an isolated place, and according to a set sequence. Rituals may be prescribed by the traditions of a community.

Prayer, music, and dancing enhance the effectiveness of ritual acts. Sacrifices and offerings help to confirm the relationship between the supreme deity, lesser deities, and humanity. Rituals take place during community celebrations and festivals for the purpose of thanksgiving, purification, and communion.

Communal Ritual

Prayer, music, songs, drums, other musical instruments, dancing, and sacrifice come together in vividly orchestrated communal rituals. These rituals celebrate such things as purification rites, communion rites, and agricultural rites.

Ritual Leaders

Ritual leaders are those members of the community who preside over and conduct particular religious rituals. They come to their leadership roles in different ways. Some positions are hereditary. Others are the result of a special spiritual calling along with special training. This category of African ritual leaders includes rulers, priests, mediums, diviners, healers, rainmakers, elders.

Liberation is a ritual in most African traditions, and libations are the pouring of a (usually alcoholic) beverage in memory of deceased friends and or family. Ancestors Venerations is an element of Kimoyo; in this chapter, I will discuss this ritual in full detail, and I will also give small examples of other African rituals.

Chapter 5 talks about Ancestors, and when most talk or think about the Ancestors, they think of pouring libations. I will not get into full detail of what Ancestor is since I already cover it.

An ancestor is a person who has been born, named with a purpose. One who has been initiated and recognized as an adult by their community, married and had children, or cared for an extended family member. One who has reached old age and became elder by living a good life. One who has died and transitions back to spiritual or Ancestor realm.

Kimani S.K. Nehusi text Libation: An African Ritual of Heritage in the Circle of Life pg.1

says libation is a ritual of heritage within the African Circle of Life. In the world view of Africa, this circle is described and represented by transformations through different stages. It states in the human journey through existence: from dwelling in the spirit world, coming into this sphere (the physical world), birth and naming, puberty, initiation, and adult, marriage and procreation, eldership, transition into the spirit world again, ancestorship, and sometimes of elevation into divinity. Each stage in this circle is marked by appropriate rituals of heritage that indicate status transformation and clarify and make smooth each process of change, thus rendering the entire journey easier. Such rites of passages including naming ceremonies, initiation ceremonies, marriage ceremonies, transition ceremonies, and rites of elevation to divinity. Liberation is an important part of each of these aspects of the African ritual and African experience.

How to Awakening the Ancestors Kofi (2010) argues that ancestors who are in the ancestral realm are divinely entrusted with man's spiritual development and have divine directives to guide and protect man. He likens the act of pouring libation to making a mobile phone call. The way the phone alerts its owner with a ringing tone is synonymous with awakening the ancestors when libation is poured.

Libation in Africa is a ritual of heritage, a drink offering to honor and please the Creator, the lesser divinities, our sacred ancestors, humans present and not present, as well as the environment (Nehusi,2015: 3).

Libation is found throughout the African world: on the continent and in the Americas, the Caribbean, and other parts of the world where Africans dwell. The significance of this ritual transcends its distribution across the immense time/space correlation that is occupied by the African experience of life. Libation is a vital part of the African cultural equipment. In fact, this ritual is a marker of African identity (Nehusi, 2015: 1).

Libation can be poured at other occasions, such as to mark the settlement of a dispute, before chopping down trees (individually or parts of a forest). At enstoolment of Chiefs, at the many festivals on the African calendar and other African spiritual gatherings. The pouring of libations can be seen in every ceremony and gathering in the African way of life.

A libation may be poured with any drinkable liquid, including water, milk, wine, beer, or strong (alcohol). However, alcohol has been the dominant choice for some generations now, especially in West Africa. More often than not, clear spirits are chosen on important occasions: gin in Ghana, clairin in Haiti, white rum in Jamaica, Guyana, Trinidad, and other places. The choice of liquid depends on the nature of the libation and prayer and what your aim is in invoking (awakening) the Ancestors.

(Tasha Davis,(2017) African Rites of Passage, https://africanholocaust.net/ritesofpassage/)

· **Water** is for cooling and healing and creating orreconciling relationships.

· **Milk** is associated with motherhood and the Divine Feminine due to most women's lactation phase after giving birth; Milk was considered a perfect offering to Creator and Spirits alike.

· **Liquor** is fiery and is usually used to rouse, cement,ignite, protect and perform strong purification.

· **Wine** is mid-way between the two and is good for friendly relations, creating fellowship between man and spirit.

African Myth or Legend About The Rise of Pouring Alcohol

The origins of the ritual of libation are so ancient and so important that even to the people of Kemet, they were obscure, lost in the mists of time, and therefore accounted for in legend and myth. In one such account of things, the sun divinity Ra retreated in anger from humans and the earth because of the latter's irreverence in plotting against him and ridiculing him because he had grown so old that he drooled. He sent his daughter, Hathor, to avenge his hurt. She decided to wipe out humanity and proceeded so well that Ra changed his mind and wanted to stop the slaughter, but Hathor's blood lust could not be easily arrested. Eventually, she was stopped by a trick. She served copious quantities of red beer, believing it to be blood, and became so drunk that she forgot about killing. So humanity was saved. In Ayi Kwei Armah's estimation, "this legend explains the rise of a propitiatory custom found everywhere on the African continent: libation, the pouring of alcohol or other drinks as offerings to ancestors and divinities."

(Armah, 2006: 207).

Not all forms of libation are poured. Sometimes libations are shared with the addition of personal Ase, which is done by SPEWING the liquid from one's mouth onto the Earth or Deity or Ancestor Shrine. This carries much strength but is not done carelessly.(If you don't know when to do it, ask a traditionalist for assistance.)

(Malidoma Patrice Some (2011) Water of Life
http://archive.constantcontact.com/fs012/1101454195791/archive/1104089676928.html)

Young people do not usually pour libation in the presence of Elders unless their youthful energy is identified as a necessity for that particular ritual or ceremony. Libation is done by community elders or the oldest member of the family. It can also be done by clergy of all ages, provided the eldest clergy present sanction and approve of the person identified.(This may sound familiar. In some church's young people ask publicly for the right to speak or preach, even when their presence has already been planned, to guarantee that the eldest among them will be supporting their efforts and firming up the spiritual energy present.)

The person officiating Libation must possess the spiritual force to open the way to Spiritual communication. We go with the safest route during this occasion and choose to allow those that are older, trained, or more versed than us to conduct such affairs.

(Malidoma Patrice Some (2011) Water of Life http://archive.constantcontact.com/fs012/1101454195 791/archive/1104089676928.html)

Examples of funeral rituals In some cultures, the body is shaven, washed, and wrapped in clothing. In the past, the body could be wrapped in animal skins or even covered with bird feathers. The Ancient Egyptians are noted for their elaborate preparation of the body of the deceased. However, the Swazi are known to squeeze the fluids out of the body to slow decay. Among certain groups of Yoruba, clothing is put on the deceased backward so its soul can find its way back to the Earth to be reborn.

Mourning Customs

Mourning rituals may continue for at least a week after the burial, and during the formal mourning period, traditional practices include:

- Not leaving the house or socializing
- Abstaining from sexual activity
- Not talking or laughing loudly
- Wearing black clothes, armbands, or pinning pieces of black cloth to the mourner's clothing
- Men and women of the family shaving their hair, including facial hair, which symbolizes death and new life

Widows are expected to mourn for six months to a year, and children who lost a parent are expected to mourn for three months. After the formal mourning, the family can stop wearing black. The family may hold a ritual or create a shrine a few days or weeks after the funeral to honor and respect their dead. At some time later, the family may hold a ceremony to commemorate the deceased becoming an ancestor.

(Kastenbaum, Robert. Macmillan Encyclopedia of Death and Dying. Macmillan Reference USA, 2003.)

SACRIFICE

The act of offering sacrifices is undoubtedly one of the most universal phenomena. Sacrifice may be defined as the "giving up" of a thing for the sake of another that is higher or more urgent. It may also refer to that which is given up for a cause or something else. From time immemorial, offering a sacrifice has been considered the proper way to approach the godhead. The goods that were offered were products from the harvest; the firstlings of the flock, flowers, or flour, were to show their gratitude and request for divine favors.

Metu (1988), African Traditional religion is strictly linked with rituals expressed in sacrifice, since it is only in a sacrifice that the Supreme Being is reached. The gods and lesser divinities appeased man's peaceful existence in the world. Ritual sacrifices, therefore, are performed for purification, oath-taking, prayer, medicine, cure or healing, increased fertility, the defeat of enemies, changing of people's destinies, warding off evil, revealing the future, and so on. Sacrifices are also offered during festivals and consecration of the living.

Awolalu and Dopamu (1979) identify seven categories of sacrifice: meal and drink offering, thanksgiving or gift offering, votive offering, propitiation or expiation offering, substitutionary sacrifices, or offering, preventive and foundation sacrifice.

Types of Sacrifice

Propitiatory Sacrifice

A diviner often prescribes this sacrifice. The Yoruba call it Ebö ètùtù. In this sacrifice, the offering belongs entirely to the deity; the sacrifice is never shared but burnt or buried. It is performed during a crisis like an epidemic, famine, drought, or severe illness. This sacrifice is also made when a worshipper violates a prohibition. For example, among the Akans, if a man indulges in sexual intercourse in the bush, Asase Yaa, the Earth goddess, has to be appeased. Among the Mendes of Sierra Leone, sexual intercourse in the bush is also regarded as a violation of Maa-nsoo, the Earth goddess. On such occasions, sacrifice should be offered at the sacred groves to propitiate the Earth's mother and the ancestors.

Preventive Sacrifice

This sacrifice is prescribed as a precautionary measure to prevent danger or disaster. For example, when a particular community learns that an epidemic is raging in a nearby village, it may offer this sacrifice to prevent the scourge from entering the village. Among the Yoruba, the preventive sacrifice is known as Ogunkoja, "that which wards off attacks." Among the

Akans, palm nuts, raw meat, and raw food are often placed at the entrance of the town or village to ward off evil spirits. Among the Yoruba, the animal victim that is slain and offered to the deity may be buried or exposed at the entrance to the town, village, or house.

Substitutionary Sacrifice

The substitutionary sacrifice has an element of propitiation and prevention. It is offered in place of the person who might have suffered some kind of misfortune. It may also be offered to avert danger or trouble that might befall someone. Among the Yoruba, usually, a sheep is used as a substitute for the human being. The sheep is rubbed against the offerer's body to transfer the illness or misfortune to the sheep. It is believed that the destiny of the offerer is exchanged, hence the name Ebo Irapada (Redemption or Exchange Sacrifice). Among the Mendes, a fowl is sometimes offered as a substitute. The leg of the chicken is broken, accompanied by words such as "We have observed this man; we see a big trouble coming on him, but now as we break the leg of this chicken (he breaks one of its legs), may it, now disabled, carry his trouble; and may the trouble return and fall on anyone who was going to cause it."

Thanksgiving Sacrifice

Generally, Africans love to express gratitude. The Yoruba articulate thanks to divinities and espouse communion with fellow human beings by engaging in ebö öpü ati ìdàpò. This type of sacrifice is usually accompanied by feasting, in which the worshippers and the divinities concerned share a communal meal.

Votive Sacrifice

The votive sacrifice is also a thanksgiving sacrifice to express appreciation to a deity and also to fulfill vows. It is a common practice among some Africans, particularly the Yoruba, the Mendes, the Akans, and the Anlo, for devotees of some divinities, to go before their divinities to pour out their minds and to promise that if their needs are met, they will give specified offerings in turn. This sacrifice is known as Ebo Eje among the Yoruba; the Akans call it abode ε (Twi), and it is known as dzadodo among the Anlos.

Foundation Sacrifice

Foundation sacrifice is offered at the beginning of projects such as the foundation of a house, starting a business, or the site of new land for cultivation. In several societies in Africa, before houses are built, or villages are founded, sacrifices are made to the gods. Among the Akans, before a building is put up, a sacrifice of appeasement is made to the Asase Yaa (Earth goddess). This sacrifice is meant to prevent evil spirits from entering the place.

Sacrificial Objects

In several African societies, sacrificial offerings include a fowl, a four-legged animal, and other things like kola nuts and palm oil. An offender in Anlo land has to offer a sheep, whereas the Mendes offers rice and palm oil and sometimes a fowl. An offender in Akanland offers a sheep or sometimes a fowl depending on the taste of the gods. What is commonly offered must be without blemish. Some of the sacrificial objects used especially by the Yoruba include obi (kola nut), epo pupa (palm oil), efun (native chalk), ataare (alligator pepper), mariwo (palm fronds), eyin (eggs), and so on.

With Sacrifice, we think of blood, especially Animal Sacrifice. Let look at what blood means to the Africans. Blood is viewed in African cultures as the source of life. In fact, almost every African culture has rituals associated with blood. For example, among the practitioners of some forms of Vodou in Benin, the priests gather their spiritual powers in a practice called lighting the fires, in which they pay homage to Ogun, the god of fire, iron, and war. During the ceremony, a cow is usually sacrificed, and the blood is spilled on the ground. Indeed, the blood of animals has been used to call forth the spirits for thousands of years in African history.

Benjamin Njie(Blak Pantha) talked about blood when he was asked about blood sacrifice during a QA part right after his lecture, and he states blood moves us all; we have blood in our bodies, arteries, veins, the different things that make our heart go, so without blood were done. Blood in the African traditions is the highest concentration of energy to have, so when you inner act with other energies, it's an energy exchange because nothing is free in life, so there has to be some type of exchange to whatever you want to happen, to happen.

Wudjua Iry Maat also added on behind brother Benjamin Njie during the QA and said if we go back in ancient time in humanity, the earliest human being, what they observe was that out of all the body fluids of the human body, when urine leaves the body, they notice the person still lived, when saliva leaves the body or sweat leave the body they saw the person still lived, but when they saw the red substance (blood) leave the body the person dies, so blood becomes a symbol of life, so, blood is used as a contract, a sealing of the covenant, so the word blood in a lot of African languages mean oath to take an oath. Many of these African traditions had a contract, a social contract with the spirit world or with other people, and they sign it with blood. People would cut themself and shake their hands or signs thing in blood; blood became important, blood was the highest form of agreement.

I can validate what both brothers said, and you all can too. Benjamin Njie(Blak Pantha) talks about there has to be some type of exchange to whatever you want to happen. Now, if we look at The Hamer people who live in the Omo valley, they have a ceremony that is called Bulah, which is bull jumping. During this rite of passage ceremony, the young Hamar boys become adults. The Hamar women also participate with the whipping ceremony. The young boy's female relative does something for them, such as getting whipping until they start shedding blood for them in exchange for their future. This meaning that if the young girls face hards times in the future, they'll remember them because of the blood they shed and the pain they went through at his initiation.

Her scars on her back from being whipped mark how she suffered for her brother. There were other examples I could have given, but I thought this was very interesting dealing with them sacrificing their back to be whipped until their blood hits the ground, to show their love for their relative in exchange for the help in the future by the young boys becoming indebted to them because they put their life on the line by shedding their blood.

Wudjau Iry Maat blood becomes a symbol of life in African Traditions. The Himba people share the same sentiment, so when we look at the Himba People who live in South Africa in the northern part of Namibia. The Himba uses their famous red ochre cream that is made by pounding the ochre stone (Hematite) into small pieces. Otjize, a mixture of butterfat and ochre that is rubbed regularly onto a woman's skin. It is also used in their long plaited hair. In this arid land where water is scarce, the Himba seldom wash with water. The mixture serves to protect and scent, clean the skin and hair and enhance their appearance, so if you see a Himba woman, her hair and skin would be red. The Himba believe that this red color is beautiful. It also has symbolic meaning as it unites the red color of earth and blood, which symbolizes life.

Hamer Girls Sheading Blooding After Whipping Cermony

Himba Girls bodies and hair cover in red ochre

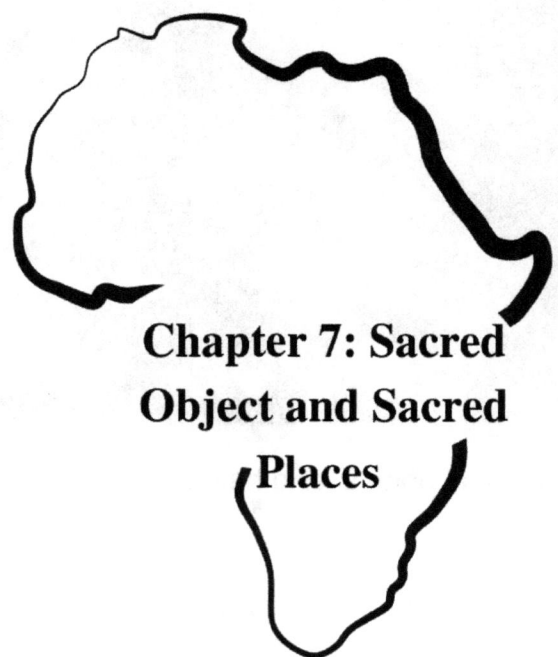

Chapter 7: Sacred Object and Sacred Places

Sacred Leader

African kingship and chiefship often serve as both spiritual and community leaders. Kingship is integral to African Kimoyo for at least two reasons. First, in the origin myths of several peoples, such as the Baganda of Uganda and the Edo of Nigeria, the first king or chief of the community was endowed with the sacred power of the Supreme Deity. At times rulers have been described as gods or as endowed with God's divinity. Second, the physical well-being of a king reflects the well-being of his people, including their agricultural and hunting life.

So, African kings, queens, and chiefs have both privileges and duties. Their position carries with it outstanding power, authority, and influence. However, rulers are endowed with power and prerogative; they are also bound by obligations and kept in check by taboos. The ruler is the father/mother of the people and the symbol of their ethnic unity. Therefore, he or she must solve human problems, give an ear to all subjects, and represent the people in contact with other powers.

Parrinder, Geoffrey. (African Traditional Religion. New York: Harper & Row, 1962.)

In many countries where Kimoyo is strong, the king is the high priest of the people. As a high priest, he is not only in charge of matters of government but also of religious matters.

High Priest

In African religious tradition, a priest is a ritual leader who oversees, administers, and coordinates spiritual matters for the community. Priests may be men or women. Priests are important figures in maintaining the religious affairs of an African ethnic group. Priests are usually attached to a temple of a god and are charged with its care. People become priests by both vocation and training.

Diviners

Diviners are ritual leaders whose special position is to unveil the mysteries of the past and future. In so doing, they pronounce what may be causing problems in the community. Diviners read the signs of the present and have techniques by which they discover hidden knowledge about the past, the present, and the future of those who consult them. To find out the unknown for a client, diviners may use shells, pebbles, water, animal entrails, and many other objects regarded as "mirrors." From these, they read why something has gone wrong.

Mediums

Mediums are people who can contact the spirit world, usually by being possessed by spirits. As a rule, they become mediums through being possessed by superhuman beings, after which they undergo training. Mediums are generally women. They are attached either to a priest at a temple or to a diviner. They sink into a trance, usually induced by music, drumming, singing, and becoming possessed. The spirit speaks through the medium, transmitting messages from the spirit world to human beings. Sometimes the message may be in a strange language, and the priest or an assistant may be called to interpret.

Healers

In some parts of Africa, a healer is called musawo, "a person with a bag." Healers are easily distinguished by the bag they carry and by their attire. Healers customarily wear amulets, shells, and other decorative accessories that ordinary people do not wear. The bag that they carry is their trademark. In it are all types of medicines. In a broad sense, healers are ritual leaders whose service relies on supernatural powers. They come to the aid of the community in matters of health and well-being. Healers work in conjunction with other ritual leaders to keep the community members physically and spiritually healthy.

What is Sacred?

The African worldview is based on a belief that every living and inanimate object is sacred on some level. Some are deemed more sacred than others. Devotees of traditional religions recognize domestic and wild animals as sacred and full of great power. Domestic animals such as dogs, goats, and roosters are often used for sacrificial purposes. Certain animal body parts—such as feathers, nails, entrails, horns, beaks, and blood—are used as offerings and divining. Many wild animals are sacred because they have wisdom and powers, because they are believed to be inhabited by spirits and because it is said that they were sent to earth by God to communicate with humans in some cases.

(Riggs, Thomas. Worldmark Encyclopedia of Religious Practices. Thomson Gale, 2006.)

Most ethnic groups believe various herbs and plants contain special powers that are useful for religious purposes. Certain herbs are sacred, and those priest specialists who have deep knowledge of how to use them are called herbalists. In addition to having medicinal uses, the herbs carry symbolic properties and qualities that make them appropriate for religious uses.

Sacred Places

Sacred places are where the rituals and rites are carried out in Kimoyo. Some of the places are constructed just for the sole purpose of rituals and rites. These sacred places were in nature where the individual or the community world go for ritual purposes. The African society or communities would go to nonsacred places on occasion to serve as ritual spaces. These are often homes in which senior family members may officiate as ritual elders.

Sacred places in nature

·Mountains

·Oceans

·Lakes

·Rivers

·Waterfalls

·Forests,

·Rocks

- Caves
- Trees

MOUNT KENYA

Mount Kenya, the highest mountain in Kenya and the second-highest in Africa after Kilimanjaro, lies just south of the equator in central Kenya, approximately 95 miles (150 kilometers) from Nairobi. It is variably referred to as "The Mountain of Mystery," "The Place of Light," or "Mountain of Brightness." It is also sometimes denoted as the "Mountain of Whiteness" because of its snow-capped peaks. Mount Kenya National Park has been designated as a United Nations Educational, Scientific, and Cultural Organization World Heritage Site. The Gikuyu (or Kikuyu—the British spelling of the word) of Kenya has a beautiful creation story that incorporates how Kere-Nyaga or Kirinyaga, the extinct volcano commonly called Mount Kenya, came to be. After a brief discussion of the sacred character of mountains worldwide, this entry describes that creation myth and the continuing importance of the myth and the mountain in Gikuyu religious belief.

Lakes embody unique qualities of water that are distinct from streams, rivers, waterfalls, seas, and oceans. Like streams and rivers, lakes are a source of precious freshwater and fish, both essential for sustaining life. However, unlike rivers, lakes are completely bordered by land that, combined with their ability to nurture and sustain life, likens them to the life-sustaining fluids of the womb. Therefore, many lakes are considered "mothers," having feminine attributes, or are connected with origins.

Lake Victoria

The Luo name for Africa's most famous lake, Nalubaale (Victoria), the second-largest freshwater lake in the world, translates as "Mother of Gods." Lubaale means deity, and the prefix na denotes the feminine. A further connection between lakes and motherhood exists in the region where Nalubaale is located, which is called the Great Lakes region of East/Central Africa. The Great Lakes region is part of the Great Rift Valley, home to the world's earliest human fossil record. Lake Nalubaale is also the source of the Nile River.

Kenny, M. G. (1977). (The Powers of Lake Victoria. Anthropos, pp. 717–733. Retrieved from http://www.pbs.org/wnet/africa/explore/greatlakes/greatlakes_overview_lo.html)

Nile River

The Nile River considered the longest river globally, is approximately 4,258 miles (6,853 kilometers) long, but its exact length is a matter of debate. Flowing northward through the tropical climate of eastern Africa and into the Mediterranean Sea, the river passes through 11 countries: Tanzania, Uganda, Rwanda, Burundi, the Democratic Republic of the Congo, Kenya, Ethiopia, Eritrea, South Sudan, Sudan, and Egypt.

The Nile has two major tributaries: the longer White Nile considered the prime stream and headwaters, and the Blue Nile carries about two-thirds of the river's water volume and most of the silt. Every year in Egypt, the Nile overflows and creates a rich valley of black soil that is abundantly fertile. This fertility was central to Egyptian civilization. With the blessing of this natural fertility, Egyptians grew a range of native crops and non-native crops, including various grains, vegetables, and fruits.

Rocks and Stones

These humble, unassuming objects manifest God, the source of creation, human life, rain, and the dwelling place of spirits in African religion. When they are combined to form massive structures, such as the Great Pyramid of Giza and the hill complex at Great Zimbabwe, they offer a powerful testament to their sacred significance.

This tradition of creating with stones is echoed in Great Zimbabwe, which means "stone house."These structures date back to AD 1085 and include more than 500 villages, with citadels and conical towers. Millions of cut stones were laid without mortar or cement. The architectural styling appears to be local with no outside influences and is unique in the world. Examples of such styling are the elliptical walls and curved lines that follow the natural landscape, created during the height of the classical period of construction. Select buildings were oriented to positions of the sun and stars, causing speculation that some of the structures may be temples. However, little is known about the symbolic significance of the structures.

(Asante, Molefi Kete. Encyclopedia of African Religion. SAGE, 2009.)

Trees have served as important symbols and spaces in African traditional religion. Although the actual significance attached to trees differs from region to region, Africans could call on a shared spiritual vocabulary that gives trees a sacred and cosmic meaning. In fact, many African creation stories designate cosmic trees as the source of all human life. Because of this association with life, trees are also linked to fertility, regeneration, and even death.

(Zuesse, E.M.Ritual Cosmos: The Sanctification of life in African Religions. Athens: Ohio University Press. 1979)

Trees were also metaphors for regeneration. Some African groups believed that the nuts, leaves, roots, or branches from trees could help cure sickness, thus regenerating those who were ill. Trees also acted as sacred spaces for the critical coming of age and initiation rites. For example, initiation into Kore ,society among Mali's Bambara cultural group involved bringing young boys into a sacred grove (a cluster of trees that performed as a site of spiritual activity). The boys would lie around the sacred tree in the center of the grove, where they would experience a regenerative second birth. After the power of the tree had regenerated them, the boys would mark the end of their childhood and their entrance into adulthood.

(Parrinder, G. African Traditional Religion.Westport, CT: Greenwood Press1962)

The Sacred Baobab Trees

We were discussing trees, so I can not leave out the sacred baobab tree that got everyone saying the baobab is the tree of life. 2019 I began to research these trees, and I can say they truly help sustain life. The baobab trees can be found in most countries in African, and the trees are common in America, India, Sri Lanka, Malaysia, China, Jamaica, and Holland. The Baobab Tree can grow to enormous sizes, and carbon dating indicates that they may live to be 3,000 years old. They go by many names, including boab, boaboa, tabaldi, bottle tree, upside-down tree, monkey bread tree, and the dead-rat tree (from the appearance of the fruit).

There are nine species of the baobab tree (genus Adansonia)

1. Suarez Baobab

2. Fony Baobab

3. Madagascar Baobab

4. Za Baobab

5. Perrier's baobab

6. Giant Baobab

7. Montane African Baobab

8. Australian Baobab

9. African Baobab

The tree also has shiny and slick outer bark. The baobab can reflect light and heat through this adaptation, keeping it cool under the savannah's unforgiving sun. Some scientists have argued that the reflective nature of the bark may help protect the tree from the impact of wildfires, which are pretty common during dry season.

The native people living near Baobab trees quickly discovered that the strange, cork-like bark of the tree is soft and fibrous. The fibers can be woven into cloth or fashioned into a strong rope. As a bonus, the tree bark is fire resistant, and so the clothing made from it also provides some protection from fire.Elephants Topple Baobab Trees in Search of Water because the large trunk of the Baobab tree is used to store water, an adaptation to its dry climate. In fact, a single tree can store up to 32,000 gallons of water. In times of drought, humans can tap into the Baobab tree to extract the water.

(Harris, Karen. Fascinating Facts About the Strange and Beautiful Baobab Tree, 25 Sept. 2018, historydaily.org/fascinating-factsabout- the-strange-and-beautiful-baobab-tree.)

It is said that griots were buried in the sacred baobab trees. Griots are considered masters of knowledge and keepers of historical records across generations. They include singers, poets, instrumentalists, musicians, and storytellers who maintain oral history in parts of West Africa.

Abdoulaye Sene, a griot from the Serer Community, explains why they put their griots in the baobab trees. "We put griots in baobabs because they are considered sages. They're the ones who reorient the community when there are problems. Griots are the repositories of knowledge. If griots are buried underground, it would be as though we were burying our history. We can't bury knowledge because it enlightens our future.

The baobab tree provides nutrition, food, medical properties, sweet fruit, and water. This tree has it all for sustaining life. African ritual places are human-made structures or marked areas at which Kimoyo rites may be observed. These include shrines, tombs, temples, and sacred localities. Since the beginning of time, Africans have sensed a great invisible power, a vital force that surrounds and is part of all nature. To help themselves come to terms with this power, Africans have devised ways of containing it by inviting it to reside in human-made places and objects to perceive it in smaller doses.

Temples

A temple is a place or a building where people congregate to worship, pray, and ask for favors from spiritual powers. There are numerous types of temples constructed in Africa according to the various traditions of different peoples. There are large temples, small ones, and even miniature ones.

Temple of Karnak

The temple of Karnak was known as Ipet-isu—or "most select of places"—by the ancient Egyptians. Located at the northern end of the town of Luxor, Karnak Temple has three main sacred areas that honor three gods: Montu, an ancient local warrior god; Amun, the chief god of Thebes; and the goddess Mut, wife of Amun. Amun, Mut, and their son, Khonsu, were members of the sacred family known as the Theban Triad.

The construction of Karnak Temple began in the Middle Kingdom and continued into the Ptolemaic period, although most of the extant buildings date from the New Kingdom. The main place of worship of the Eighteenth Dynasty Theban Triad with the god Amun as its head.

Tombs

The tradition of tomb building in Africa goes back millennia, including tombs such as the pyramids of ancient Egypt and Nubia. Helping us trace back some vital religious ideas, the Great Pyramids at Giza express belief in the king's divinity as representative of the Sun god Re and the place where he ascended to join the Sun god in the afterlife. There are many other representative types of religiously expressive tombs, the Kasubi Tombs of the Kabakas of Buganda in Uganda. These tombs are tended by young priestesses, who keep the fires within them and perform rites that worshippers may attend. The tombs thus serve as places where ordinary people may be in touch with the higher powers.

(Lugira, Aloysius M. African Traditional Religion. Third ed., Chelsea House, 2009.)

Shrines

Shrine is a word of Latin origin, which means a box used to contain a precious or sacred object of worship or veneration. The term is generally expanded to include buildings and places such as churches, temples, mosques, and cathedrals. The African cosmological concept of a shrine is much more expansive. Thus, it could include animate and inanimate objects such as rivers, buildings, rocks, lakes, mountains, or trees. African cosmology suggests that a shrine would not merely be a means of containment for some sacred or precious object or deity but comprises the essence of that which the African deems divine and worthy of worship and veneration. Because Africans conceptualize the universe and its entities as a composite whole, it is difficult to separate the shrine from the entity it represents or contains. African shrine activities include prayers, libation, sacrifices, divination, offerings and consultations, and other sacred events. African shrines vary in form and location. They are generally constructed of natural materials found in nature. They can be found inside the African home, the African compound, the African village, and other venues such as forests or river banks. African shrines are usually maintained by trained priests, priestesses, or family elders.

(Mbiti, J. African Religions, and Philosophy. New York: Anchor Bay.1970)

African shrines are often dedicated to deities representing families, lineages, vocations, clans, and stratification levels. Africans construct shrines as vehicles of an interface between the practitioners and the divine entity, focusing on their worship/veneration. Shrines may also serve as a sanctuary for both animals and human beings .

(Mbiti, J. African Religions, and Philosophy. New York: Anchor Bay.1970)

Objects

African art is a central part of Kimoyo expression and, in the African worldview, is known for its powerful ability to represent abstract ideas and spiritual forces. African artists produce sacred icons and symbols of kimoya in an enormous array of forms, both abstract and figurative. Traditional artists typically carve images that express God's powers, demigods, ancestors, and spirits as intermediaries between deities and humans. A royal stool may depict powerful animals such as leopards and tigers.

Practitioners of kimoyo are generally familiar with the symbols and icons. Still, only a few trained individuals can interpret the significance of such symbolic and iconic forms, which imply religious meaning in initiation, divination, and secret societies.

Now let go to Southeastern Nigeria with Igbo People and Tanzania and Mozambique with Makonde people and look at art expression dealing with deities and initiations. In the Igbo Traditions, that is called Odinani, and the lesser deities are called the Alusi, each of whom are responsible for a specific aspect of nature or abstract concept. According to Igbo belief, these lesser alusi, are elements of Chukwu the supreme deity, and they have their own specific purpose. Alusi manifests in natural elements, and their shrines are usually found in forests in which they are based around specific trees. At shrines, íhú mmúọ, an object such as a hung piece of cloth or a group of carved statues are placed at an alusi's group of trees to focus worship.

Deities are described as 'hot' and often capricious so that much of the public approach shrines cautiously and are advised to avoid them at most times, and priests are entrusted in the maintenance of most shrines. Many of these shrines are by the roadside in rural areas. Tender palm fronds symbolize spiritual power and are objects of sacralization; shrines are cordoned off with omu to caution the public of the deities presence. Larger carved and clay modeling's in honor of an alusi also exist around forests and rivers. Other alusi figures may be found in and around people's homes and the shrines of dibia; much of these are related to ancestral worship.

Makonde people traditional rituals for as initiation of boys and girls into manhood and womanhood demanded carved objects. The girls are usually given a carved wooden doll to carry it around with them on their bodies as a good-luck charm. The boys have to fight a mapiko masker as part of the circumcision ceremony.

Makonde sculptors carve characters recounting stories, and they outline their facial expressions and features accordingly. When representing their people, they create harmonic sculptures with fine features, while their enemies are represented with distorted and ridiculous features and a grotesque look. Traditional Makonde statues portray women as they represent the birth and the survival of the Makonde. Their breasts and stomachs are highlighted, especially the typical scarifications on the forehead, cheeks, and over the mouth. Lizards are engraved on the sides of the abdomen since these animals are thought to increase fertility in women.

Chapter: 8
Music

Music in Africa is another element in kimoyo, so in this chapter, we will discuss dance, songs, and drums. No matter what African people were doing, there was always music involved.

African dance occupies a central place in cultures throughout the African continent, embodying energy and a graceful beauty flowing with rhythm. In Africa, dance is a means of marking life experiences, encouraging abundant crops, honoring kings and queens, celebrating weddings, marking rites of passage, and other ceremonial occasions. Dance is also done purely for enjoyment—ritual dance, including many dances utilizing masks, to achieve communication with the deities. African dance has also adapted, filling new needs that have arisen as many African people have migrated from villages toward the cities.

Now, most traditional African dances have to be divided into four major categories, which are "ritual dances," "ceremonial dances," "communal dances," and "griotic dances" (dances expressing local history).

Ritual Dance

Ritual dance the most ancient African dance there is. Ritual dances are initiated by the inform and the elders. They are usually religious in nature and are designated for specific occasions that expedite and facilitate the most powerful expression of Africa People.

Here a side not about ritual dancing in Africa. The people can not perform unless they have a big understanding of Kimoyo. Individuals frequently participate in several distinctive forms of worship; they are not perceived as conflicting in any way. They are considered cumulative means of achieving the same result, which is improved the quality of life. In chapter 5, we learn Ancestor veneration is normal in African societies and is an important element in Kimoyo. We will look at the Chewa People from Malawi, southeastern Africa, and see how dance is included in venerating their Ancestors.

Gule Wamkulu

Gule Wamkulu, or big dance, is the best-known and longest dance of the Nyau. It is also known as pemphero lathu lalikulu la mizimu ("great prayer to our ancestors") or gulu la anamwaliri ("dance of the ancestors"). Before the Gule Wamkulu dance, Nyau dancers observe a series of secret rituals associated with their society, a secret brotherhood. The dance is mainly performed at funerals and memorial services but also initiations and other celebrations. The masks worn by the dancers on such performances are in the form of animals or "beasts" such as antelopes believed to capture the soul or spirit of the deceased that brings renewed life. The purpose of the dance is to communicate messages of the ancestors to the villagers and make possible continued harvests and continued life. Nyau is a protection against evil and an expression of religious beliefs that permeate society.

Ceremonies Dances

Ceremonial dance is performed at weddings, anniversaries, rites of passage and coming of age celebrations, the welcoming of visitors, the culmination of a successful hunt, and other happenings shared by the whole tribe. The ceremonies dances are also expressing the community more than the mood of an individual or a couple. In Villages throughout the continent, the sound and the rhythm of the drum express the people's attitude. The drum is the sign of life; its beat is the heartbeat of the community.

We will discuss the importance of the drum later on in this chapter but right now, let's talk about the Karo people of the Omo Valley in Ethiopia.

At the end of the harvest and at times of initiation and marriage, the Karo people come together to enjoy dances. During the moonlight dances, the Karo men leap, joining one another in long lines towards the women, who come forward one by one to select the man whom they favor. Afterward, Karo men and women, coupling themselves, perform rhythmic and pulsating dances, thrusting their hips one against the other in the dusty atmosphere of early evening. These dances often lead to marriage after the initiate has been successful. A Karo man may take as many wives as he can afford, but usually, he marries only two or three.

Griotic Dance

The Griot, the village historian, teaches the village about their past culture and traditions. Traditions and stories are kept in the form of music and dance, containing elements of history or metaphorical statements that carry and pass on the culture of the people through the generations. Griotic dances not only represent historical documents, but they are ritual dramas and dances. They tell stories of historical events.

Communal Dances

Communal dances express the life of the community, not and an individual. The communal dance and ceremony dance have the same thing in common, where dances occur with the community or village alone with singing and drumming. The drum is the sign of life; the drumbeat is the heartbeat of the community. Such is the power of the drum evokes emotions and touches the souls of the community.

Dance is used as a recreational entertainment that edifies social patterns and values. Dance is and also an important element in the people's way of life call Kimoyo. Each tribe and community has its own signature dance moves for diverse events. They dance when a child is born; a bride is prepared, a prayer for better rains, rejoice of better crops, curse evil, and even ward off diseases and danger. Dance was a way of life and incorporated in everything. Were there were drums there dancing, where there was singing there was dancing.

Drums

African Drums is one of the oldest instrument in the world. They served as musical instruments, objects for ceremonies, and as a method of communication. The drums were part of everyday lives, and others held special significance giving power to their owner or created to honor ancestors. In many instances, the traditional African drums are connected to spiritual endeavors and medicinal purposes. The drums also had roles in ceremonies, such as births, weddings, funerals, rights of passage, rituals, ancestors, lower deities, creator/supreme being, war, initiations, sacrifices, and festivals. Today, drums continue to be used in African life. They are played at weddings, festivals, and dances throughout the world. There were many variations of traditional African drums, and the most mention drums were the Ngoma drum, the Talking Drum, Kpanlogo Drum, and Djembe Drum.

Traditional African drums are typically made of wood, rope, twine, and various animal skins (i.e., goat, cow, calf, and antelope). The perishable nature of the materials used to construct drums during antiquity inhibited their survival. The various shapes of African drums reflect their perspective categories:

These include cylindrical and conical drums, barrels, hourglasses, waisted drums, goblet, and footed drums, long drums, frame drums, friction drums, and kettledrums.

African drums are generally played with the hands or a combination of the hands and a striker, such as drumsticks, mallets, or leather straps. Some African drums are played with the feet or a combination of the hands and feet. Music is an integral part of every aspect of life among African people. Africans employ music in their everyday lives, whether at work, play, or worship. In most instances where one finds African music, the drum is present.

("African Drums." Contemporary African Art, www.contemporary-african art.com/africandrums.html.)

From culture to culture, who plays traditional African drums varies. In some tribes, only those with a hereditary right to be a drummer are allowed to play the instruments, while among other peoples, drums were the one instrument that anyone in the village could play. The drummer was often believed to become possessed by the spirits of the drums – those of the drum maker, the animal whose skin was taken for the drumhead, and the tree from which the wood came for the making of the drum's shell.

We just mention that most drums are made out of wood that comes from trees, and the drummer is believed to become possessed by the spirit of the drum. Some rituals took place before the cutting down of a tree and the wood used to make the drum. In our iAw wrt(great elder) Rkhty Amen Book A Life Centered Life Living Maat page 28 states: Here is an interesting ritual that was described to the author by a Ghanaian artist named Kwame Nkrumah. He related that when the drummer sets out to make a drum, He first considers the innate spirit of the tree(source of his wood). The tree is alive and therefore sacred.

Before the tree falls and is chop up as wood, he pours libation and begs forgiveness for this act. This act is done not only for the tree but also for the sake of the drum so that the spirit/energy of the tree will enter the drum. Thus the man links his work of making the drum with the spirit world. When the drum is made, the drum for him is alive. The Drum will speak to the people. When the drum is finished, a ritual called Ayane is played to awaken the drum; it is music to please the spirits. People will use the drum to do good.

Talking Drums

Talking drums are African drums whose pitch can be regulated depending upon how the drummer strikes the sound of the drum and changes its tension. These pitches can mirror those of a person's voice, and thus, the drums are called "talking drums" (ikenga-Metuh, 1987). In Mali, for example, the drums have historically been used for four primary purposes; first, they are used by Jellis or griots charged with orally recording, preserving, and sharing their community's histories and culture (Gehman, 1987).

The Jellis used the drums as memory devices to help them remember important people and events. Second, talking drums are used to communicate messages across distances and villages (Mbiti, 1971). A king or other political authority may send a drummer throughout his land as a messenger.

The drummer plays or beats his drum, and because the villagers know the "language of the drum," they understand if the king is issuing a warning, a celebratory invitation, or some other news (Mbiti,1969). Third, talking drums are also used during religious rituals; ; jellis and griots ran these ceremonies and used the talking drums for celebration and sacred rites and stories. Fourth, talking drums are used to bring people together and help settle disputes among village members (Hobley, 1910). The drums are now used more for celebration and entertainment than for communication. Yet, Jellis continue to be respected by members of the society and are considered keepers of African, especially Mali tradition. In many African cultures, the talking drums are the cultural instruments that have endured and survived generations. In Nigeria, for instance, talking drum is used in notifications or alerts and entertainment in palaces and most ceremonies.

Djembe Drum

It is widely believed that the Djembe (pronounced JEM – Beh) has its origins with the "numu", a social class of professional blacksmiths from the Mandinka (Maninke) people of western Africa in around 1300 AD. It is believed that they were the first to carve this wooden instrument. It is said that the term "djembe" originates from the Bambara saying "Anke djé, anke bé," which translates to "everyone gathers together in peace."

African history isn't written down for the most part but is passed down through stories and traditions. The origin story of the djembe is no different, and there are multiple stories of how this popular drum came to be.

Example of one myth

'Long ago, before humans knew of the drum, it was owned by the chimpanzees, who played it in the trees. At that time, there was a great trapper named So Dyeu. The chimpanzees would often come near his camp. One day So Dyeu spotted them eating fruit and entertaining themselves with the drum. He said, 'This thing they are beating is beautiful, I will set a trap,' so he dug a hole and laid a snare. The next day he heard a great commotion and the sounds of the young and old chimpanzees crying. He went to investigate and found the chimpanzee drummer caught in the trap. So Dyeu captured the drum and returned to the village, where he gave it to the village chief.

The chief said, 'We have heard the voice of this thing for a long time, but no one has seen it until now. You have brought it to us; you have done well.' and in return, the chief gave his first daughter to be So Dyeu's first wife. So the chimpanzees no longer have the drum, and that's why they can only beat their chests.

(Blanc, Serge. African Percussion: the Djembe. Percudanse Association, 1997.)

The djembe is primarily the instrument of dance used at marriages, funerals, and circumcisions. Songs are also played during the plowing, sowing, and harvest, used for courtship rituals and even to settle disputes among the men of the village.

In west African society, specific instruments such as the balafon, the kora, and the ngoni are subject to hereditary restrictions. This means that only members of the griot caste (historian/storyteller) may play them. The djembe is not a griot instrument, and there are no restrictions on who may become a djembefola.

In daily life, various events are accompanied by unique songs and dances. The griot usually performs these, accompanied by drummers, singers, and dancers. Songs tell of great leaders, like King Sundiata, or praise certain professions, like the cobblers or hunters.

In a typical ensemble, the griot is accompanied by two djembes and a dunun player. So you see, drums were used in everything that the Africans did. Drums are a part of Kimoyo in every way, i.e., ritual, prayer, sacrifice, rites of passages, and libations' pouring. The drums were also used as a communication tool to send messages far away or locally throughout the villages.

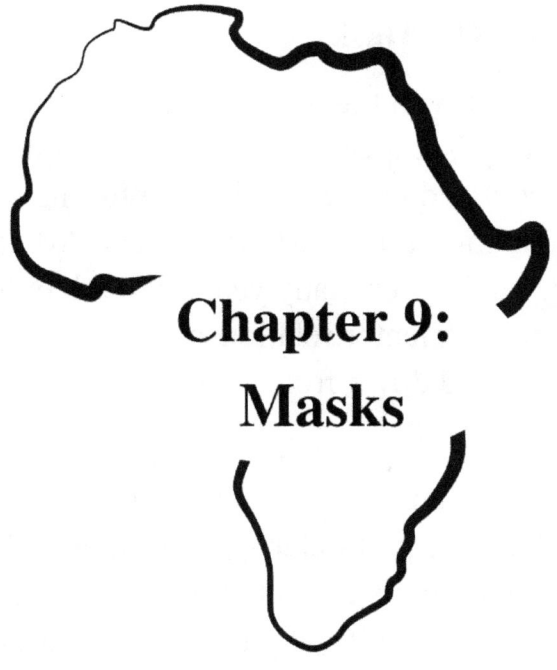

Chapter 9: Masks

In Africa, masks are essential and worn in every element of Kimoyo. The Masks are designed to ward off evil spirits, prevent ill heath, preventing disasters, bring rain, bring children to married couples, ceremonies, rituals, policing, government, social control, community affairs, initiating, and sometimes entertainment.

Maker Of The Mask

Let start first with the mask maker; and the mask maker is a specially educated person who is respected and feared by his tribe for his understanding of the spirit world. The Artist's training can last for many years through either an apprentice/mentor relationship or by skills that are passed down from father-son.

An artist trained in woodcarving makes the mask. During an apprenticeship, the artist learns about the particular styles of masks that are important to his community. A mask carver is always male and usually holds an important status among his people.

A mask is often made from a single piece of wood. The artist uses an ax-like tool called an adze to create the features on the mask. Fine details are carved on the mask using a knife. To darken or add color to the wood, an artist may soak the mask in mud, burn it, rub it with oil, or paint it with natural pigments or manufactured wood stains. An artist will often make the mask in private. After the artist completes the mask, an elder will perform a ceremony to allow a spirit to inhabit the mask and give it power. Likewise, when a mask is no longer used, the elder performs a ceremony to remove its power.

(Stelzig, Christine. Can you Spot the Leopard? African Masks (New York: Prestel, 1997)

Masks can be grouped into three main forms:

- face masks
- helmet masks
- headdresses

Face Mask

The face mask is the most common form and usually curves over the masker's face, stopping right before the ears. Other face masks, often described as plank masks, are completely flat.

Helmet Mask

A helmet mask covers the entire head and sits on the shoulders of the masker.

Headdresses

The headdress rests on top of the masker's head, and it helps to disguise the masker's identity. A costume made of raffia or grass is attached to a headdress to cover his or her face.

Some masks take the shape of humans. These masks often have stylized features to represent ideal beauty and strength. Other masks take the form of powerful animals that are important to the community, such as an elephant, antelope, or hawk. Sometimes masks combine attributes from different animals or even combine human and animal features. When thesefeatures are brought together on a mask, the powers of each also are combined. Masks are also decorated with animal hair, straw for hair and beards, animal horns, animal teeth, feathers, and seashells. The horns represent the growth of millet, legs roots of the plants, while ears represent songs that women sing in the harvest time.

Biombo masks are usually carved from wood and colored with red "tukula" powder, a dye made from the camwood tree. The eyes are a typical coffee bean shape. A triangular checkerboard design is used to decorate the eyebrows and the planes of the face. The three forms at the back of the head represent the Biombo hairstyle. Feathers are often attached to the top of Biombo masks and are worn during tribal rituals and ceremonies. The Biombo live south of the inter-section of the Lulua and Kasai rivers in the Democratic Republic of the Congo.

Senufo masks are created by specialist artists who live apart from the rest of their village. Senufo masks combine the features of animals and humans in a single design. The Senufo artists have a high status in their society as their masks and sculptures are believed to have the power to help communication between the living and their dead ancestors. Senufo masks are used in the rites of the Poro society, a male organization that educates young men in the traditions and responsibilities necessary for their coming of age.

The Senufo worship their ancestors, particularly Kolotyolo - the 'Ancient Mother' who holds so much power that she must be carefully approached through intervention by lesser gods. The Senufo are a farming people of over 1,000,000 that stretch across various bordering countries in West Africa, including the Ivory Coast, Ghana, Burkina Faso, and South Mali.

Bwa masks are believed to possess special powers which are controlled by those who wear them. These masks are plank-shaped with a circular face at one end and a crescent moon at the other. Their wearer looks through a hole in the mouth. The eyes are based on an owl, and the hooked nose comes from the hornbill. Both these birds are thought to possess magical powers. The plank section is decorated with geometric patterns, an essential design element in many African masks and carvings. The geometric pattern creates an external rhythm that echoes the internal spiritual energy of the artwork. It can also be used as a coded language where the design communicates secret knowledge to those in the know.

The designs on this Bwa Mask, which is used to celebrate boys' initiation into adulthood, represent information about the myths and morality that the boys must learn before they can be accepted into adult society.

The Yohure are noted for their beautifully crafted masks that combine human and animal features. They have elaborate hairstyles, which often include horns, elongated faces with a high forehead, arched eyebrows, and a low protruding mouth. The front of a Yohure mask is outlined with triangular zigzag designs.

Yohure masks are used in dance rituals to help villagers come to terms with the death of one of their people. The masks represent the Yu spirits who restore the social balance after a bereavement.

These masks are considered very powerful and dangerous objects. They must be kept out of sight of women for fear of the effects that the supernatural powers of the Yu spirits may have on them.

The Yohure live in the central region of the Ivory Coast to the east of the city of Bouafle.

In this chapter, we have learned how Africa uses masks for various events ranging from ritual ceremonies to social events without a religious connection. Masked dancing can serve educational purposes, passing on important cultural traditions, Masks or the event may be purely theatrical, providing entertainment for the community. But regardless of its function, the African mask becomes powerful only when it takes action with costumes, music, dance, and storytelling in front of a gathered audience. Like theatre, it only exists in motion as a community interaction.

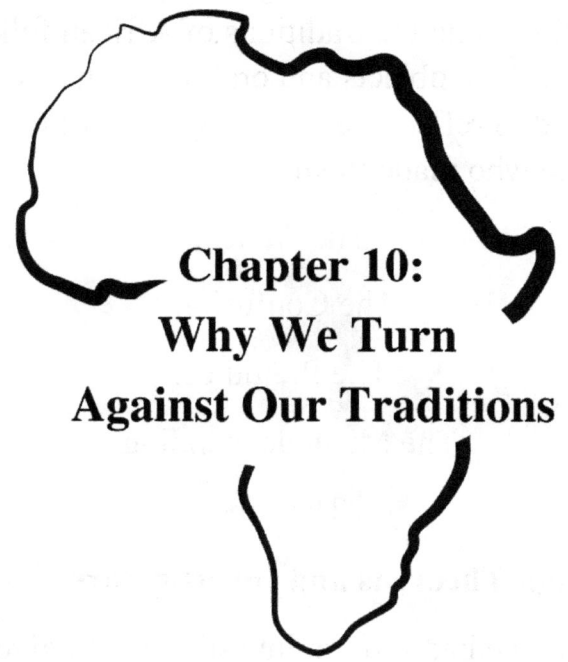

Chapter 10: Why We Turn Against Our Traditions

Before Invaders, foreigners, Arab enslavers, European enslavers, Colonialists, Missionaries, African people have had their own way of life, traditions, or what they are calling present-day religion, many years pre any of those names above. The existence of those religions is evident in ancient African art, particularly in rock engravings, paintings, sculptures, buildings, and the traditions of African folklore. Both artistic objects and oral traditions were created to reflect the religious fabric of the people who made them.

The Attack,

The Confusion,

The Prejudice,

The Misunderstanding ,

The Lies

Foreign Theorists and Investigators

Before we had foreign investigators to give the world an idea of what the religious beliefs of the Africans looked like, there were theorists who have never been in Africa but who regarded it as the "Dark Continent" where people had no idea of God and where the Devil in all his abysmal, grotesque and forbidden features, armed to the teeth and with horns complete, held sway. These theorists had fantastic tales to tell about Africa. And one such tale was recorded in a Berlin journal which Leo Frobenius read before he ever visited Africa to see things for himself. Among other things, it said:

Before introducing genuine faith and higher standards of culture by the Arabs, the natives had neither a political organization nor strictly speaking any religion. Therefore, in examining the pre-Muhammadan conditions of the negro races, to confine ourselves to the description of their crude fetishism, their brutal and often cannibal customs, their vulgar and repulsive idols, and their squalid homes (Frobenius, 1913: pg. 12).

And similar to this was the dialogue that took place between Edwin Smith, who had gone out as a missionary to Africa, and Emil Ludwig , an eminent biographer. When Ludwig got to know that Edwin Smith was in Africa as a missionary, he was surprised; and in his surprise, he asked, "How can the untutored Africans comprehend God? Deity is a philosophical concept in which savages are incapable of framing"(Pritchard, 1965: Pg. 1)

These two quotations show the ignorance, prejudice, and pride of these theorists. They did not know, and they never confessed their ignorance about Africa and the Africans. Hence Professor Idowu strongly describes this period as the "period of ignorance and false certainty" in the study of African Traditional Religion (Idowu, 1978: pg.88).

Western scholars attempting to write off Africa as a spiritual desert, "there were, undoubtedly, a few who had the uneasy feeling that the story of a spiritual vacuum for a whole continent of peoples could not be entirely true."While some scholars admitted that the whole of Africa could not be a spiritual vacuum, they raised doubt as to whether the God that the Africans believed in was the "real God" or their own God.

They started coining expressions like "a high god" or "a Supreme God." A. C. Bouquet, for example, seemed to be expressing the Western mind when he said, "Such a High God hardly "differs from the Supreme Being of the 18th century Deists, and it is absurd to equate him with the Deity of the Lord's Prayer"(Heffer, Cambridge, 1933, p.106).

Here we see that Bouquet is propounding a theory of many Supreme Beings in order to place the African God at a lower level than the Deity that he (Bouquet) met in Jesus Christ. This is an intellectual attitude complete with racial pride and prejudice (Awolalu,1976).

Several investigators were interested in finding out the truth about religion in Africa. Even here, we should remark that not all of them took the trouble to make thorough investigations. Some of them did their research part-time, e.g., the Colonial Civil Servants, the missionaries, the explorers, etc. Others were anthropologists and sociologists who examined religion just by the way, and yet others were theologians and trained researchers. Several of them did their investigations as best as possible among the peoples whose languages most of them did not understand. Even when interpreters were used, one could not be sure that the interpretation would be accurate (Hutchson, 1858). The missionaries were particularly subjective, and they could not see anything good in African Traditional Religion. The impression they had of it was that it was not worth knowing and expected that the religion would soon perish. But they were proved wrong (Myovela, 2014: pg. 24)

Misleading Terms

ATR's (African Traditional Religion) religion was described with many racial and misleading terms by missionaries, anthropologists, historians, sociologists, and archaeologists to belittle African Traditional Religion or Kimoyo. Again such terms include animism, savagery, paganism, magic, fetishism, idolatry, juju, primitive, heathenism, and polytheism, ancestral worship. It should be noted that these terms are still widely used by both African and non-African writers and researchers. Some African writers have been westernized by Europeans hence they also use these racial and misleading terms whether knowingly and unknowingly in describing African traditional religion.

We need to examine some of these words and bring out their connotations.

(1) Primitive: The New Webster Encyclopedic Dictionary defines primitive as the beginning or origin; original; first; old fashioned; characterized by the simplicity of ancient times."

(2) Savage: The dictionary meaning is about the forest or wilderness; wild; uncultured; untamed

violent; brutal; uncivilized; untaught; rude; barbarous; inhuman." In one word, savagery is the opposite of civilization.

Just looking at the definition of savage its says untaught, rude, barbarous, and most Europeans use these terms when describing Africa culture and traditions. As I look back in history, those terms definitely apply to European culture and their ancestors. You, the reader, will see the meaning of savage is opposite of civilization, meaning Africans were uncivilized, but how could that be, cause when I look at their history, I see they build great cities/civilizations pre Arab and Pre Europeans.

(3) Fetishism: Earlier in this paper, we came across Frobenius, who claimed to have read a Berlin journal where it was stated that Africa was a place dominated by crude fetishism. What does fetish mean? Linguists claim that the word is of Portuguese origin. The early Portuguese who came to Africa saw that the Africans used to wear charms and amulets, giving the name feitico to such things. This is the same word as the French fetiche. The dictionary meaning of fetish is any object, animate or inanimate, natural or artificial, regarded by some uncivilized races with a feeling of awe, as having mysterious power

residing in it or as being the representative or habitation of a deity, hence fetishism is the worship of, or emotional attachment to, inanimate objects. But Rattray corrected this wrong notion of the early investigators when he said:

Fetishes may form part of an emblem of god, but fetish and god are distinct and so regarded by the Ashanti. The main power, or the most important spirit in a god, comes directly or indirectly from Nyame, the Supreme God. In contrast, the power or spirit in a fetish comes from plants or trees, and sometimes directly or indirectly from fairies, forest monsters, witches, or from some sort of unholy contact with death; a god is the god of the many, the family, the clan, or the nation. A fetish is generally personal to its owner. We see, then, that it would be entirely wrong to describe the religion of Africa as fetishism. There may be an element of this in the dayto-day life of the Africans, but it is incorrect to describe it all as fetishism (Rattray, 1923:pg.24).

(4) Juju: The word juju is French in origin, and it means a little doll or toy. Its application to African deities has been perpetuated by English writers.

For example, P. A. Talbot in his Life in Southern Nigeria, devoted three chapters to Juju among the Ibibio people and discussed the various divinities among them. How can divinities, however minor, be described as toys? Africans are not so low in intelligence as to be incapable of distinguishing between an emblem or symbol of worship and a doll or toy. Juju is, therefore, one of the misleading and derogatory terms used by investigators out of either sheer prejudice or ignorance.

(5) Paganism and Heathenism: We choose to treat paganism and heathenism together because the meanings applied to them are similar, if not identical. The word pagan is from the Latin word paganus, meaning peasant, village, or country district; it also means one who worships false gods, a heathen. But when the meaning is stretched further, it means one who is neither a Christian, a Jew, nor a Muslim.

On the other hand, Heath is a vast track of land; and a heathen inhabits a heath or possesses the characteristics of a heath dweller. According to the New Webster Encyclopedic Dictionary, a heathen is, a pagan; one who worships idols or does not acknowledge the true God; a rude, barbarous and irreligious person.

These words are not correct in describing the indigenous religion of Africa because the people are religious, and they do believe in the Supreme Being. If the only religious people are the adherents of Christianity, Judaism, and Islam, then all the other world religions become either heathen or pagan and uncivilized! Presumably, these terms are used in an attempt to distinguish between enlightenment and barbarity. What has this to do with religion? We think such terms are more sociological than religious (Awolalu, 1976).

(6) Animism: The great advocate of the theory of animism was E. Tylor in his Primitive Culture. Many writers still describe African Traditional Religion as animistic. This means attributing a living soul to inanimate objects and natural phenomena. From our own study of the African Traditional Religion, we find there are unmistakable elements of animism. For example, the Iroko tree is not an ordinary tree, and It is believed to be inhabited by a spirit. The Oshun River (in Western Nigeria) is believed to be more than an ordinary river because the spirit (Oshun) dwells in it, making the river productive in many respects, especially during barrenness.

Lightning and thunder are manifestations of the thunder god (Awolalu, 1976).

I should add that it would be a gross error to label African traditional religion as animism since every religion has some form of belief in the existence of spirits. For example, Christians believe in the existence of the Holy Spirit. Shintoists believe in the existence of Kami {spirits}. Jews believed that Yahweh inhabited mount Horeb. Muslims venerate the Sacred Stone, the Ka'ba in Mecca when they go for pilgrimage, and among the Hindus and Jains, it is believed that spirits inhabit natural objects (Omoregbe, 1993). In short, to say that African traditional religion is animistic would be misleading and racial.

(7) Idolatry: Idolatry is derived from the Greek word eidoloatria or eidolon, which means the worship of an image, figure, or shape, usually copied from the real thing (Harper, 2009; Kano, 2014). Thus with regard to African traditional religion/Kimoyo, it was used by mainly European Christians who speak of ATR/Kimoyo as the worship of false gods. Jebadu (2006) also notes that idolatry is the worship of the creature instead of the Creator, and creature worship is made by people who are a creature.

This is where foreign scholars get it wrong. Omoregbe (1993) explained that when an African prays before a statue, image, or sculpture, he or she is not talking to or worshipping the statue or the image in question, but the divinity (the Supernatural Being) symbolically represented by that statue. This corroborates with the view of Awolalu that the statue or emblem of worship by African people is not a means to an end in itself; it is only a means to an end.

If, for example, a piece of wood representing Obatala (a Yoruba deity) is eaten by termites, the worshippers of Obatala will not feel that their god has been destroyed by the termites, because the piece of wood is only a symbol, serving as a visible or concrete embodiment of that which is symbolized.

The "idols" seen in the religion are symbols that represent the deity and absolutely meaningless apart from its spiritual connotations. For example, if a statue or sculpture representing Antoa Nyamaa (Asante deity) is destroyed possibly by a natural disaster. The worshippers of Antoa will not feel that their goddess has been destroyed because the piece of the statue is only a symbol, serving as a visible embodiment of what is symbolized.

Symbolic representation is not peculiar to African traditional religion/Kimoyo, but to other religions such as Christianity, Buddhism, Shintoism, and so why is Idolatry only attributed to the religion of African people? It would be grossly unfair, misleading, and racial to describe the religion as idolatry. At the same time, the images of Mary and Jesus in the Catholic Church have not turned Christianity into an idolatrous religion.

Nana Osei Bonsu, B.Ed. (2016) African Traditional Religion https://www.researchgate.net/publication/331474122_African_Traditional_Religion_An_Examination_of_Terminologies_Used_for_Describing_the_Indigenous_Faith_of_African_People_Using_an_Afrocentric_Paradigm

(8) Polytheism: "In West Africa," said Parrinder, "men believe in great pantheons of gods which are as diverse as the gods of the Greeks or the Hindus. Many of these gods are the expression of the forces of nature, which men fear or try to propitiate: These gods generally have their own temples and priests, and their worshippers cannot justly be called animists but polytheists since they worship a variety of gods (Parrinder, p.24)

What is so heartbreaking to me is that we, the African Americans who are descendants of

Africa, use these same derogatory terms. I have heard quite a few of those derogatory terms personally in my lifetime. I guarantee it want be my the last because I am from the bible belt, so anything outside Christianity theology is demonized. Most of our brothers and sisters do not know our Ancestors got introduce to their faith Christianity via trade, invasions, slavery, and missionary work. A lot of brothers and sisters would argue that Christianity has always been in Africa, which is false. Now let's look at some of the entry points of Christianity with King Ezana in East Africa and King Nzinga in Central Africa.

The adoption of Christianity in Ethiopia dates to the fourth-century reign of the Aksumite emperor Ezana. Aksum's geographic location is in northern Ethiopia. The kingdom was located along major international trade routes through the Red Sea between India and the Roman empire. The story of Ezana's conversion has been reconstructed from several existing documents, the ecclesiastical histories of Rufinus and Socrates Scholasticus. Both recount how Frumentius, a youth from Tyre, was shipwrecked and sent to the court of Aksum. Frumentius sought out Roman Christian merchants, was converted, and later became the first bishop of Aksum. At the very least, this story suggests that Christianity was brought to Aksum via merchants. Ezana's decision to adopt Christianity was most likely influenced by his desire to solidify his trading relationship with the Roman Empire. Christianity afforded the possibility of unifying the many diverse ethnic and linguistic peoples of the Aksumite kingdom, a goal of Ezana's leadership.

Christianity, at its entry point in ancient Central Africa, testifies to the presence of African religion since ancient times. In 1491 King Nzinga of the kingdom of Kongo in Central Africa converted to Christianity through contacts with the Portuguese adventurers. He encouraged the Kongo nobility and peasants to follow his example. African Christianity lasted in Kongo for 200 years. The strength of African religion accounts for the swift embrace of Christianity by the Kongo kingdom.

In African religion, a king is not only a ruler; he is also a religious leader. When their king converted to Christianity, it was apparent that his subjects would follow suit. The highly centralized and hierarchically structured society helped information flow throughout the kingdom. Christian doctrine was easily translated into Kikongo, the local language. Concepts like god, spirit, and holiness are easily found equivalents with concepts in Kongo religion. Portuguese missionaries helped establish a spirit of cooperation.

Colonialist Times

The Portuguese exercised navigational prowess along the western and eastern coast of the African continent. What they saw of African religious practice in coastal areas led them to conclude that Africans worshipped fetishes. The interior of Africa, however, continued to remain a mystery to Europeans. Stories about the Mountains of the Moon, suppositions about raw materials in the interior of the continent, and pagans who remained unconverted attracted much speculation and attention in Europe. The situation encouraged Europeans to consider exploring the interior of Africa. Between 1768 and 1892, 10 European explorers went to Africa. Seven of these were British, one was French, one was German (working for the British government), and one was Anglo-American. Europeans learned about Africa from the explorers, and this knowledge led to European ideas about colonialism. (The term colonization refers to acts of settling on a given piece of land, while colonialism is the system in which a nation imposes its authority over other peoples' territory.) The European scramble for Africa that ended in the Berlin Conference of 1884–85 arbitrarily divided Africa among European colonialist powers. Colonialism left all parts of African native cultures, including religion, fractured and bleeding.

Under colonialism, African belief systems and modes of thought became subjects of ridicule. Explorer Samuel Baker was among those who thought that African belief systems did not even exist. In an 1867 article ("race of the Nile Basin"), he said, "Without any exception [Africans] are without a belief in a Supreme Being, neither have they any form of worship or idolatry; nor is the darkness of their minds enlightened by even a ray of superstition. The mind is as stagnant as the morass which forms its puny world. Some colonialist administrators spoke with disgust about Africans, whom they called "these incurably religious" folk. Some missionaries wished to destroy what they thought of as devilish and superstitious beliefs and replace them with what they considered true religion.

During colonialist times African religion was thought of as a "less-than" religion on a par with paganism, fetishism, primitive religion, and animism. Before and during the times of colonialism, African religion was dismissed as unimportant to modern society's development. And even to those with less critical views, African religion was often tolerated rather than accepted.

Islam has not always been in Africa neither. It enters the Africa interior around the 7th century with the Arabs. The Muslim Conquest of Egypt 641AD-654AD and Egypt was the gateway into African for the Arab. Islam spreaded to West Africa via the Mauritania route. Africans were enslaved by the Arab and force to convert or die. Many African tribes converted to Islam on their own because Islam provided economic benefits. Economic benefits were not the only reward associated with Islam conversion, nor did economics play a role in all instances of conversion.

For many centuries we have been convinced and influenced by foreigners, i.e., those outside of Africa, that our roots and Ancestors way of life is satanic, demonic, and pure evil. This is because of the stereotyping and the prejudice, negative rhotic that has been pass down to us via the Arab slave, European slave trade, missionary work, colonialization, and western educations through their schools. This has caused us to reject and turn our backs on our roots. We have to un-learn and re-learn. We have book stores, online books stores, and the internet where information is at our fingertips, so there is no excuse not knowing where you come from, what your forefathers and foremothers practice, taught, learned, gave, and their contributions to the world.

2012 I had no clue about where I came from, African culture, traditions, languages, history, accomplishments, or contributions. It wasn't until 2013 I began to want to know more after an exchange I had with a brother online. I have been studying indepth for eight in a half years. I have bought tons of books; I have taking classes, listening to tons of interviews by African Scholars, and talk for hours on the phone or via social media with those who practice the traditions, those who sat at the feet of some of our famous and world-renowned master teachers. Few years after my studies, I became interested in the Yoruba people traditions call Isese in Nigeria. I tried to practice it on my own because there where no Ile (Temple) in Mississippi. I stop trying to practice it on my own after my brother Benjamin Njie got initiated into Isese and started to show us and share with us what we been reading is not correct and accurate information on the Yoruba people's indigenous traditions Isese.

Later I found myself loving all of the traditions in all parts of Africa and realized that I didn't have to practice just one pacific one, so I took elements from many of them. African traditions are very similar but different.

A couple of years ago, I started researching the origin of African Traditional Religion or Kimoyo. After studying and researching and verifying some things, I truly understand the psyche of the people in African thousands of years ago and why they came up with the different elements that make up Kimoyo. Our Ancestors fill in the blank of the unknown through their folktales, legends, folklore, myths based on their experiences, and the natural phenomenon from mother nature. Those concepts for their traditions were bases on their geographical location.

When you study all cultures worldwide, their traditions and culture are based on their experiences and geographical locations. The people begin to ask questions and answer their questions by explaining the unknown in the best way they knew how. By me studying the origins of what people calling religion, way of life, way of the Ancestors, African traditional religion, or Kimyo has made me an agnostic. An agnostic is a person who believes that nothing is known or can be known of the existence or nature of God or anything beyond material phenomena; a person who claims neither faith nor disbelief in God.

Biography

•Mbiti, John S. African Religions & Philosophy.Heinemann, 2006.

•Idowu E. Bọlaji. African Traditional Religion: a Definition. Fountain Publications, 1991.

•Frobenius, Leo. The Voice of Africa, Tr. Rudolf Blind, Vol. 1. Hutchinson, 1913.

•Ensminger, J. (1997). Transaction Costs and Islam:Explaining Conversion in Africa. Journal of Institutional and Theoretical Economics (JITE) /Zeitschrift Für Die Gesamte Staatswissenschaft,153(1), 4-29. Retrieved April 17, 2021, from ://www.jstor.org/stable/40752982

•Ross, Emma George. "African Christianity in Ethiopia." In Heilbrunn Timeline of Art History.New York: The Metropolitan Museum of Art, 2000- http://www.metmuseum.org/toah/hd/acet/hd_acet.ht m (October 2002)

•Stelzig, Christine. Can you Spot the Leopard? African Masks (New York: Prestel, 1997 Blanc, Serge. African Percussion: the Djembe. Percudanse Association, 1997.

- Amen, Rkhty. A Life Centered Life Living MAAT. Rkhty Amen, 2012.

- "African Drums." Contemporary African Art, www.contemporary-african art.com/africandrums. html.

- Lugira, Aloysius M. African Traditional Religion.Third ed., Chelsea House, 2009.

- Harris, Karen. Fascinating Facts About the Strange and Beautiful Baobab Tree, 25 Sept. 2018, historydaily.org/fascinating-facts-about-the-strangeand-beautiful-baobab-tree.

- Parrinder, G. African Traditional Religion.Westport,CT: Greenwood Press 1962

- Zuesse, E.M.Ritual Cosmos: The Sanctification of life in African Religions. Athens: Ohio University Press. 1979

- Asante, Molefi Kete. Encyclopedia of African Religion. SAGE, 2009.

- Kenny, M. G. (1977). (The Powers of Lake Victoria.Anthropos, pp. 717–733. Retrieved from http://www.pbs.org/wnet/africa/explore/greatlakes/ greatlakes_overview_lo.html

- Riggs, Thomas. Worldmark Encyclopedia of Religious Practices. Thomson Gale, 2006.
- Kastenbaum, Robert. Macmillan Encyclopedia of Death and Dying. Macmillan Reference USA, 2003.
- Malidoma Patrice Some (2011) Water of Life http://archive.constantcontact.com/fs012/1101454195 791/archive/1104089676928.html
- Tasha Davis, (2017) African Rites of Passage, https://africanholocaust.net/ritesofpassage/)
- Nehusi, Kimani S. Libation: An Afrikan Ritual of Heritage the Circle of Life. UPA, 2015.
- "Elders ." Encyclopedia of African Religion, by WadeW. Nobles, SAGE, 2009, pp. 236–238.
- Lynch, Patricia Ann, and Jeremy Roberts. African Mythology: A to Z. 2nd ed. New York: Chelsea House, 2010. Sundara, Oscar. Serer Religion. Duc, 2012.

- World Affairs Council of Houston. "The Oral Traditions of Africa." Teach African, static1.squarespace.com/static/53cfd0e5e4b057663ea1bc61/t/57b1e0b746c3c406dd172afd/1471275383444/Oral+Traditions+of+West+Africa.pdf.

- Asihene, Emmanuel V. Traditional Folk-Tales of Ghana. Edwin Mellen Press, 1997.

- Finnegan, Ruth H. Oral Literature in Africa. Oxford Univ. Press, 1993.

- Fadeiye, J, D.(2004). Historiography and Methods of Teaching History for N.C.E and Undergraduates.Oyo

- Agorsah , Kofi E. Religion, Ritual And African Tradition: African Foundation . Author House: Illustrated , 2010.

- Pickrell, John. "Timeline: Human Evolution." New Scientist, 4 Sept. 2006, www.newscientist.com/article/dn9989-timelinehuman- evolution/.

Fu-Kiau , Kimbwandende. Self Healing Power and Therapy: Old Taeching from Africa . Africa Tree Press , 2014.

- MacGaffey, Wyatt "African Traditional Religion" 06 May 2016, https://www.oxfordbibliographies.com/view/docume nt/obo-9780199846733/obo-9780199846733 0064.xml#:~:text=Parrinder%20in%201954%20and%20later,Proponents%20of%20African%20Traditional%20Religion.

- Awolalu and Dopamu (1979).West African Traditional Religion Nigeria: Onibonje Press and Boos Limited.

- Stoner, John. Makonde. Rosen Pub. Group, 1998.

- Anizoba , Emmanuel Kaanaene. Odinani : The Igbo Religion . Trafford Publishing , n.d..

Available Now
www.kofipiesietv.com

Available Now
www.kofipiesietv.com

Kofi Piesie

www.ingramcontent.com/pod-product-compliance
Lightning Source LLC
Chambersburg PA
CBHW051930160426
43198CB00012B/2093